The Research
Experience in Nursing

The Research Experience in Nursing

Jill Buckeldee

and

Richard McMahon

CHAPMAN & HALL
London · Glasgow · New York · Tokyo · Melbourne · Madras

Published by Chapman & Hall, 2–6 Boundary Row, London SE1 8HN, UK

Chapman & Hall, 2–6 Boundary Row, London SE1 8HN, UK

Blackie Academic & Professional, Wester Cleddens Road, Bishopbriggs, Glasgow G64 2NZ, UK

Chapman & Hall Inc., One Penn Plaza, 41st Floor, New York NY10119, USA

Chapman & Hall Japan, Thomson Publishing Japan, Hirakawacho Nemoto Building, 6F, 1-7-11 Hirakawa-cho, Chiyoda-ku, Tokyo 102, Japan

Chapman & Hall Australia, Thomas Nelson Australia, 102 Dodds Street, South Melbourne, Victoria 3205, Australia

Chapman & Hall India, R. Seshadri, 32 Second Main Road, CIT East, Madras 600 035, India

Distributed in the USA and Canada by Singular Publishing Group Inc., 4284 41st Street, San Diego, California 92105

First edition 1994

© 1994 Chapman & Hall

Typeset in 10/12 pt Palatino by Best-set Typesetter Ltd., Hong Kong
Printed in Great Britain by St Edmundsbury Press, Bury St Edmunds, Suffolk

ISBN 0 412 44110 1   1 56593 193 9 (USA)

A catalogue record for this book is available from the British Library

Library of Congress Cataloging-in-Publication Data

The Research experience in nursing / edited by Jill Buckeldee and
    Richard McMahon. — 1st ed.
        p.   cm.
    Includes index.
    ISBN 1-56593-193-9
    1. Nursing—Research—Methodology.   I. Buckeldee, Jill.
II. McMahon, Richard, 1960–
RT81.5.R45 1994
610.73'072—dc20   93-35414
                                                                CIP

∞ Printed on permanent acid-free text paper, manufactured in accordance with ANSI/NISO Z39.48-1992 and ANSI/NISO Z39.48-1984 (Permanence of Paper).

Contents

Notes on contributors

Having obtained a degree in History from Reading University, **Ann Bergen** commenced nurse training at Addenbrooke's Hospital, Cambridge. After hospital clinical experience, particularly in the care of the elderly, Ann became a district nurse, also studying part time to obtain a diploma in Nursing and then a MSc in Nursing at King's College, London. In 1990 Ann became a lecturer in Nursing Studies at King's College. Her particular interests relate to the care of terminally ill people in the community and the general area of integrating theory with practice.

Contact address: Lecturer, Department of Nursing Studies, King's College, Cornwall House Annexe, Waterloo Road, London SE1 8TX.

Jill Buckeldee obtained a BSc (Hons) in Nursing at Hull University and then worked clinically on medical wards and in nursing research. She then entered community nursing. Whilst working as a district nurse she studied part time for a MSc in Nursing at King's College, London. Currently Jill is a Senior Nurse in district nursing in Oxfordshire. Her interests include examining how district nurses interact with their clients, providing supportive and critical working environments, exploring ways of obtaining consumer feedback and views about community services and exploring methods of working effectively with carers of clients in the community. She is currently researching this latter area for a PhD.

Contact address: Senior Nurse, District Nursing, Faringdon Health Centre, Coxwell Road, Faringdon, Oxon SN7 7EZ.

Sophie Hyndman graduated in Human Sciences from the University of Oxford. She then went on to the University of

London where she completed a PhD on Housing and Health. From 1989 to 1991 she worked as a Research Officer for the Royal College of Nursing Standards of Care Project evaluating a quality assurance system for nurses. She is now working as a Research Associate in the Health Services Research Group at the University of Cambridge Institute of Public Health.

Contact address: Research Associate, Department of Community Medicine, University of Cambridge, Level 5, Addenbrooke's Hospital, Hills Road, Cambridge CB2 2QQ.

Judith Lathlean is Professor of Education in Nursing and Director of the General Nursing Council Trust Nurse Education Research Unit, Department of Educational Studies, University of Surrey. She is a behavioural scientist, with an extensive career in health care, social welfare and education research. Since 1979 she has focused more specifically on issues related to the education of nurses and her main publications are to do with post-registration education and training. Her particular interests currently include the study of professional education – primarily in respect of nurses, teachers and social workers – and the development of research methodology, especially action research and qualitative approaches.

Contact address: Professor of Education in Nursing and Director of the GNC Trust, Nurse Education Research Unit, University of Surrey, Guildford, Surrey.

Richard McMahon trained as a nurse at St Thomas' Hospital in London. He completed his MA from the University of Warwick whilst working at the Oxford Nursing Development Unit. His thesis for his PhD is examining the nursing role in a particular skin problem, and he has a number of other research interests including patient care at night and the care of stroke patients. He is currently Clinical Director for General Medicine at the Horton General Hospital NHS Trust in Banbury.

Contact address: Clinical Director for General Medicine, Horton General Hospital NHS Trust, Oxford Road, Banbury, Oxon OX16 9AL.

Jane Miles obtained her initial degree in Nursing from Sheffield City Polytechnic and subsequently her Masters degree in

Nursing from King's College, London. She gained most of her clinical experience in elderly care in Oxford and then took up a post as Research Tutor at Berkshire College of Nursing and Midwifery. Currently Jane is Regional Nurse for Palliative Care Services (Oxford Region) and her research interests are focused primarily on cancer survivorship.

Contact address: Regional Nurse for Palliative Care Services, Oxford Regional Health Authority, Old Road, Headington, Oxon OX3 7LF.

Ken Nolan is Course Director, Diploma in Nursing Studies at Coventry and Warwickshire College of Nursing and Midwifery. Following a broad clinical career, he became a nurse teacher specialising in health and social welfare. He has been guest lecturer at a Swedish college of health and was formerly a member of the Open University Steering Group in Nursing Development.

Contact address: Course Director for Diploma in Nursing Studies, Coventry and Warwickshire College of Nursing and Midwifery, Clifford Bridge Road, Walsgrave, Coventry, West Midlands.

Alison Richardson graduated from the University of Wales College of Medicine with a Bachelor of Nursing (Hons) and a Registered General Nurse Certificate in 1985. She has worked clinically with cancer patients since starting her career both in Wales and at the Royal Marsden Hospital in London. Alison studied part time for a MSc in Nursing at King's College, London, graduating in 1989. Her present post as a Macmillan Lecturer in Cancer Nursing and Palliative Care was taken up in 1990. She is currently registered for a PhD, examining the experience of fatigue in chemotherapy patients. Her other more general interests include exploring ways in which teachers of nursing can facilitate clinical practice at a basic and advanced level and supporting the professional carer, particularly in relation to death and dying.

Contact address: Macmillan Lecturer in Cancer Nursing and Palliative Care, Department of Nursing Studies, King's College, Cornwall House Annexe, Waterloo Road, London SE1 8TX.

Jane Robinson began her nursing career in the 1950s in Birmingham. Following various clinical nurse posts she entered health visiting, practising as a health visitor before becoming a health visitor manager and then a health visitor tutor. Prior to taking up her post at Nottingham, Jane was Director of the Nursing Policy Studies Centre, University of Warwick, for four and a half years. Currently she is Professor and Head of Department of Nursing and Midwifery, Faculty of Medicine, University of Nottingham. Jane has researched diverse areas including child abuse, health visiting evaluation, perinatal mortality, nurse management, staffing and the role of support staff and research for policy and policy for research in nursing education. She sees her current professional identity as both a nurse and a health policy analyst.

Contact address: Professor and Head of Department of Nursing and Midwifery, Faculty of Medicine, Queen's Medical Centre, Nottingham NG7 2UH.

Kath Ross started her career in nursing in Manchester and then Leeds. Following experience as a registered midwife she entered nurse education where she has remained. Kath has worked in various roles in education including curriculum development, implementing conversion courses and teaching RGN students. Following an MA in sociological Research, Kath became a Senior Lecturer in the Department of Health Care Studies at Oxford Brookes University. She teaches undergraduate nurses and paramedics research, applied sociology and introductory aspects of nursing and health care. Her interests mirror her teaching subjects and also include the development of nursing theory and women's career patterns.

Contact address: Senior Lecturer, Department of Health Care Studies, Oxford Brookes University, Academic Centre, John Radcliffe Hospital, Off Headley Way, Headington, Oxon OX3 9DX.

Acknowledgements

The idea for this book originated several years ago with discussions among our friends, colleagues and peers. We are very grateful to all those people who stimulated and encouraged our thoughts, eventually leading to this book being published.

We would also like to thank all those who have helped with this book, particularly the contributors, many of whom have struggled with the style or content but all of whom have revealed a little of themselves in order to present real accounts of their work. We sincerely hope that this will stimulate others to share their experiences in order that we may all benefit. We also appreciate the prompt submission of their material.

Finally Jill would like to thank husband Robert for his support and humour throughout the writing of the book, which ensured its completion, and Olivia whose birth during this time was distracting but meant that the whole experience was unforgettable. Richard would like to thank Kath, Clare, Hannah and Elliot who provided patience, humour and perspective during the preparation of the book.

1

Introduction

Jill Buckeldee and Richard McMahon

ABOUT THIS BOOK

Ideas for books often seem to develop over a period of years or months, either from the absence of a text that the author would him or herself find useful or from a gradual realization that there is a message that needs sharing which others would find interesting and helpful. The idea for this book arose some years ago from the early research experiences of the editors whilst completing their separate Masters degrees. We both needed to find out about the practice of research in a relatively short time and, as is common practice, relied on textbooks and lectures to give us the understanding that we felt that we required. Although there were many nursing research texts available, the instructions on fulfilling the research process were very clearcut and seemed to describe an ideal version of the process, in which few problems and difficulties arose; almost like a recipe book where, if you follow the steps correctly the dish will turn out like the picture – or not, if you are a novice. As novice researchers we experienced both trivial and fundamental problems in our projects, for which descriptions and solutions were missing from the traditional nursing research books.

Through talking to others who were trying to learn how to perform research, it became clear that we were not alone in experiencing such problems. Hearing the 'warts and all' accounts of projects performed by experienced researchers and having the opportunity to discuss these with the investigators in seminars was helpful and heartening to us. This, in association with an understanding of the difficulties encountered by fellow students, slowly led us to recognize that both novice and expert researchers would find a collection of such experiences of value.

We were aware, of course, that such a collection had precedents which we ourselves had found valuable. For example, Bell and Roberts (1984) provide a series of accounts of sociological research, including the account of a nurse, which graphically portray the actuality of research in that field. A wise, frank and humorous account of many years of nursing research is provided by Lisbeth Hockey (1985) who demonstrates that success is frequently the result of overcoming a number of pitfalls and, among other things, warns others of things that she would have liked to have been warned about herself. Both these books illustrate another point. Whilst, by their very nature, traditional research textbooks often seem turgid and difficult to read, the accounts by Bell and Roberts and by Hockey are extremely readable, having an immediacy which at times instils a feeling of suspense in the reader, which made them refreshing as academic texts. We felt that producing a readable, if not entertaining, nursing research book would be a major achievement.

It is our belief that there is not only a theory–practice gap in clinical nursing and in nurse education, but also in nursing research. By asking both novice and experienced researchers who have used different paradigms and methodologies to investigate nursing to recount their experiences, we hope to both demonstrate that gap and at the same time to start to bridge it. Whilst the specific problems and challenges described here may often be unique to that particular project, it is our belief that it is not only reassuring to know that others have difficulties and are forced to apply solutions which are either not in, or contradictory to, the traditional textbooks: also that such explanations demonstrate that it is permissible and often necessary to do so. Indeed, it is hoped that all novice researchers benefit from some degree of supervision and as with mentors to students on the wards, it is hoped that such supervisors can put the theory of research practice into context of the reality of the field.

It is not too remarkable to us that the theory–practice gap in research exists when one considers that the published research report is the medium by which research studies are normally communicated to others. This cornerstone of the academic journals both in nursing, and in many other disciplines, traditionally contains a sanitized account of the project which may dispassionately describe a few difficulties encountered, but phrased in such a way as to give little benefit of the researcher's experience to the reader. For example, in a randomized controlled trial to test the effectiveness of administering enemas to women in labour, Romney (1982) states that 'As it became clear that after 50 deliveries the trial could not be run with strict adherence to the protocol because midwives were drawing their own conclusions, the study was concluded at this point'. There is clearly an extremely valuable experience behind that statement, but there are no more than two sentences of explanation within the report. It is not unreasonable to think that researchers dare not dwell in too much detail on their mistakes or difficulties for fear of damaging their academic credibility or reputation. Indeed, we suggest that the traditional research report in which one tries to demonstrate how well one has followed the 'recipe' for that type of research (be it a randomized controlled trial or a grounded theory approach) not only stifles the sharing of creative work and often puts researchers into positions that they find morally difficult, but also perpetuates the myth that most projects follow the steps described in the textbooks without much difficulty.

We expect this book to be read mainly by people involved in some way in nursing research. However, we believe that it is not inappropriate for this book to appear on the reading lists of courses aimed at the professional development of practising nurses. Too often research is viewed as irrelevant or inapplicable by clinical nurses; it is seen as elitist, making full use of complicated terminology and jargon which alienates and confuses the uninitiated (Reed and Robbins, 1991). This book is not a collection of such 'highbrow' articles; rather, it demonstrates that those involved in research experience frustrations and pressures in their own practice and that they wish for their work to be accessible to a wide audience. Indeed, much published research is often the result of nurses' efforts to acquire academic qualifications at Masters level or above. Yet, these are often the researchers' first serious attempts at performing a study and inevitably such studies are not performed with the same skill and expertise as if they had been undertaken by an experienced researcher.

At the doctoral level, there remains an issue that to some extent the researcher is still learning about the practice of research and it is only at the post-doctoral level that one might expect a person who has learnt about research by climbing the academic ladder to be a competent researcher. Yet nursing's academic journals publish many studies that have been performed as part of a Masters or doctoral programme. This is not in itself problematic, as in the main research is worthless unless it is disseminated. However, it defies belief that behind the perfect accounts of projects given in journal articles there are not extremely valuable stories of the research experience.

THE PREPARATION OF NURSE RESEARCHERS

The way that we prepare nurses to practise research is fraught with problems. Undergraduate nurses who are expected to understand, appreciate and implement research clinically are sometimes expected, either individually or in groups, to perform a small project which often involves their peers as the respondents. It is easy to equate this approach with the culture in nursing and nurse education of experiential learning. However, as with any learning by doing, the amount of skill and knowledge gained is dependent on the student's reflection on the experience, assisted by a knowledgeable facilitator who is able to ask the student the right questions. It seems likely that such students receive far less supervision than post-graduates who are, on the whole, more independent and self-motivated. In some areas undergraduates are not allowed to perform or are discouraged from performing any sort of project which involves collecting primary data. This decision arises from worries regarding the moral position of letting students gather primary data which will almost never be collected or analysed with sufficient rigor to produce useful findings. Therefore such students do not gain the insight into research that doing a project would give them; however it is not necessary for students to graduate in nursing with skills in performing research, only in appreciating and implementing it.

Although research has become a central focus in both pre- and post-registration courses, the focus needs to be on identifying problems that require further investigation and on critiquing existing research so that its relevance in informing and changing practice can be assessed. We believe that the channelling of students' energies into the integration of research into practice would be more valuable than trying to teach them research skills which they are unlikely to use again. If research could become interwoven with practice, this may well promote a spirit of enquiry resulting in more nurses asking questions and seeking answers relating to clinical issues.

Certainly both consumers and producers of research need to work collaboratively to ensure the continued growth of nursing research. One way this could be achieved could be by extending the relatively new concept in nurse education of the lecturer practitioner. 'Researcher practitioners' could hold posts in clinical practice with a defined research component. The holders of such posts would not only demonstrate that 'researchers' are not 'better' than or dissimilar to nurses whose role is wholly clinical, but would also be able to assist in bringing research into practice and clinical problems to the attention of researchers. It would also bring home to researchers the importance of communicating their findings and conclusions in such a way that the relevance and practical implications can be easily assimilated by clinical nurses; something that we have not always done in the past (Hunt, 1987). Such developments are reliant on managers actively developing a research oriented environment and an awareness that although research can be expensive, it is an investment in the future which may well enhance dynamism in the workforce.

The way in which inexperienced researchers could make a significant and more ethically acceptable contribution to the field of research is through performing replication studies. It is fair to say that only a very small minority of research projects that take place ever get replicated. This problem is not unique to nursing; however, it is something for which nursing research has been justifiably criticized (Ecock-Connelly, 1986). Yet replication is a very good way of establishing the validity of a study and of ensuring that the results still apply some years later. For example, in the point prevalence study of skin problems beneath the breasts of inpatients, which was carried out in 1989 (McMahon, 1991), one in ten women were found either to have an active lesion or to have had one during that admission. To check the reliability and generalizability of that result it would have been helpful to replicate that study in another health authority, or the same health authority some months later. Now, some years later when there are many fewer patients in psychiatric beds and hospital based continuing care facilities for the elderly, a replication of the study would almost certainly produce a different result.

The advantage of letting inexperienced researchers gain experience through the replication of other studies rather than commencing a totally new project is that much of the groundwork, for example in the testing of research tools, has already been done. Although the experience would not be problem free, it could well avoid some of the major problems that the original researcher had to overcome. It would not be inappropriate for it to become established practice for the replicating researcher to have a tutorial with the original investigator, in order to hear the real account of the project, like those in the chapters of this book. Such an approach to the teaching of research would lead to it being established which research results one may currently have confidence in and which are of dubious value. The application of meta-analysis* to studies which used almost identical methods would be relatively easy, giving greater sensitivity to the statistics through effectively increasing the sample size. There would be less diversity in the research activity of the profession, but the robustness of findings which come from studies which may have been replicated two or three times would be extremely high.

THE CONTENT OF THE BOOK

Throughout the book some of the theoretical, practical, ethical and methodological issues in nursing research are highlighted. However, by their nature such 'true' accounts can be very personal, complex and messy. Indeed, the contents of the chapters of this book contain many points and issues which would be out of place in a traditional research report. They are, to some extent, the accounts that would normally be shared verbally on a one-to-one basis or in a seminar. The style is deliberately not the conventional academic one, so as to convey

---

* 'Meta-analysis refers to the statistical manipulation of results of separate studies, the purpose being summarisation and synthesis.' (Abraham *et al.*, 1987)

that these are not 'scholarly' works in the traditional sense of the word. We have tried to introduce a degree of intimacy into the accounts and a number of contributors expressed a feeling of vulnerability without the third person of the academic style to protect them. We hope that the bravery of the contributors in publishing these honest and, on occasions, painful accounts will be recognized and respected by the readers.

Although each contributor has a theme based on a different aspect of research it is important to realize that the aim is not to provide the necessary theory and principles to allow the reader to perform that aspect of research, but rather to encourage critical reflection and to stimulate debate on the experience described. Similarly, it was not intended to provide chapters on all types of research or parts of the research process; instead, examples from a broad range of both are presented. Many other chapters by other contributors could have been commissioned as, like Bell and Roberts, many friends and colleagues disclosed that they had experiences that they could contribute to the book when they heard about it. This further affirmed our feeling that there is a wealth of issues that surround the experience of undertaking research which could stimulate fruitful debate. So although this book is by no means comprehensive we hope that it will bring the issues raised into a wider arena and encourage others to publish real accounts of the research experience.

One of the most fundamental decisions when undertaking a study is defining the research question, the adequacy of which can determine the success or otherwise of a piece of research. In Chapter 2, Jane Miles describes her experience of defining and refining the research question for a dissertation prepared as a requirement for an MSc in Nursing. She provides an account of the difficulties associated with even deciding an area of interest for the study and the feelings of desperation that accompanied it. The fact that she only had one day per week for one year constrained and influenced her choices, particularly the availability and accessibility of samples and the need for her topic not to require approval from her local health authority ethical committee. Jane found that the problems did not stop once she had defined her area of enquiry as 'creativity'. Rather, she had the challenge of clearly defining and articulating what creativity has to do with nursing in order to con-

vince others of the need for such a study. Overall the chapter
illustrates that, like many researchers, Jane started off with a
broad question which was not measurable but through repeated
reading, discussion and debate a complex yet well-defined and
researchable question was eventually articulated. This process
is shown to be a journey of discovery and a problem solving
exercise in itself, leading to false starts and disappointments as
well as good ideas.

In Chapter 3 Judith Lathlean describes the complexities of
the processes involved in deciding upon a research design.
Judith demonstrates how this can be influenced by the funding
body and how, with a methodology such as action research,
there may be many different interpretations of that approach.
Through her account of a ward sister's training project, Judith
gives real insight into the constant need to make difficult decisions as the study progresses and at times revisit the decision
making process in choosing the methodology to monitor that it
is still valid.

In Chapter 4 Ken Nolan shares his experience of gaining
access to a sample. Research involving people with AIDS and
HIV is important, but also fashionable. Ken reveals how he had
to gain the trust of the 'gatekeepers' of the potential sample by
demonstrating his genuine interest in them before they would
give him information about potential participants for his study.
Another group of gatekeepers who had to be overcome were the
ethics committee who, in predictable fashion, were unwilling
to sanction a sociological study of people with AIDS. Having
overcome these hurdles a whole new set of problems emerged,
not least from trying to interview men for whom anonymity was
a far higher priority than for most respondents in a research
project.

Alison Richardson's account of piloting a study which explored the self-care behaviours initiated by patients to control
chemotherapy induced nausea and vomiting (Chapter 5) illustrates the complexity of such a project. Once she had identified
the overall aim and scope of the study, Alison had to embark
on a number of different phases of development to the original
design and research instruments. Four phases of pilot work
were completed which not only clarified the variables being
examined, but also confirmed the use of diaries as an acceptable method for recording self-care behaviours adopted by

these patients. Alison's work clearly demonstrates the crucial role of pilot study work in ensuring the most appropriate and effective collection and measurement of the research data.

In Richard McMahon's chapter he describes his experience of conducting a randomized controlled trial into an aspect of nursing practice. Although many scientists consider the experiment to be at the apex of the research methods tree, it can be an approach which is beset with difficulties. Richard came up against restrictive attitudes from medical and laboratory staff which seriously compromised the study. Having adopted an approach which allowed five different interventions to be tested at the same time, Richard had to confront challenges such as whether it was possible to introduce the concept of 'blinding' into a trial where it was nursing therapies, not drugs, which were being compared.

The experience of interviewing carers in their own homes is described by Jill Buckeldee in Chapter 7. She shows how this seemingly straightforward method of data collection requires highly complex skills and the taking into account of numerous considerations from choosing the setting to deciding how to terminate the interview. Several ethical issues are identified, notably the problem of conflicts between the researcher and nurse roles when many carers verbalized feelings not acknowledged or previously considered. The dilemma of what the researcher should or can do is described. In terms of conducting the interviews, Jill illustrates that too much data can be as problematic as too little and that the skills required for interviewing can be learnt and do improve with critical reflection. Finally, the therapeutic effects of interviewing for carers, many of whom are socially isolated, are clearly demonstrated.

Ann Bergen employed multiple data collection methods to explore the nursing care received by cancer patients and their relatives. She explains in Chapter 8 how her expectation that data from multiple sources using different methods would converge to answer her research questions was not fulfilled, but how she used her divergent findings constructively. Triangulation is becoming a popular method in nursing research and the decisions made by Ann in presenting her data may well provide comfort to future researchers adopting this technique.

By describing in Chapter 9 her experience of analysing qualitative data, Kath Ross shows how the reality can differ greatly from the linear process described in many textbooks. Kath graphically describes her experience of handling data from 18 indepth interviews with nurse educationalists examining their decisions to enter the field of education. Kath shares her feelings of being overwhelmed by the volume of the data, the difficulties involved in making sense of the data within time constraints and how she finally managed to escape from the mire.

Sophie Hyndman, who was one of the team involved with the evaluation of the Royal College of Nursing's Dynamic Standard Setting System, gives a good insight into some of the problems that can beset a large, multicentre project. In particular, Sophie demonstrates the problem of evaluating the influence of one aspect of ward activity when a great number of variables influence the outcomes for patients. Sophie identifies confounding variables arising from both inside and outside the wards involved in the study from patients and staff to the timing of data collection and experimenter bias. Finally, she confronts the perennial problem of the influence of conducting the experiment itself on the dependent variables being measured.

The issue of ownership of research projects, and their findings, is a complex one, especially when the results do not fulfil the expectations of those commissioning the study. In the final chapter Jane Robinson shares her experience of having carried out participant observation into perinatal mortality in one health district, only to have the report embargoed by the chairman of the authority. Her reactions to that event are shared and the sensitive (as they were perceived to be) findings explored and put into context. Jane's work concludes by describing clearly the lessons for the future that her experience has given her and of which novice researchers should be aware.

THEMES

Whilst this book may be dipped into, examination of all the chapters does prompt a recognition of a number of recurring themes identified by the researchers. Perhaps one of the most surprising to the novice researcher is that of the constraints and controls placed on the projects by outside agencies. The politics of the research process is a subject not often approached in conventional textbooks on research. Yet skill in recognizing the power and motivating variables was a crucial part of a number of the studies described. For example, both Judith Lathlean and Jane Robinson found the influence of their respective funding agencies to be considerable, either in determining the design of the studies or in controlling the dissemination of the results. It can be necessary, where researchers are employed to perform particular studies, for those individuals to balance their own beliefs and values about the research and its subject against loyalty to their employers. However, at the time of employment it may not be clear what the motivation for funding a particular project by a particular agency is, or how it may react under particular circumstances relating to the results.

The power and politics of research extend further than issues relating to funding. For example, the role of 'gatekeepers' (people who have authority to grant or deny access to potential participants in the research) in facilitating or blocking research is fundamental and it is only by fully understanding the values and motivation of these people and organizations that their support can be won. In his study of people with AIDS, Ken Nolan not only had to persuade an ethics committee but also the officers of AIDS organizations who could put him in contact with potential informants who had AIDS. Both these sets of gatekeepers were reluctant to sanction the research for the clear reason of protecting the subjects. It was only by using considerable skill that Ken was able to gain the trust and confidence of these people in order for his research to proceed.

However, ethical committees do, of course, serve a vital function as Chapters 6 and 7 illustrate. Both Richard and Jill found that it would have been very easy to persuade people to take part in their respective studies and to impart very personal information, highlighting their potential vulnerability as subjects of research. Ethical committees determine the potential beneficial and detrimental effects on participants of each study and also whether the likelihood of a study to generate or confirm knowledge is sufficient to allow it to take place.

Burgess (1984) points out that it is not necessarily people at the top of the organization who are the gatekeepers. Indeed, whilst it is true that once a researcher has the sponsorship of the person at the top of an organization people at other levels tend not to obstruct the research, many organizations do not work on the basis of a single pyramidal hierarchy. This is certainly true in health care; in his chapter Richard McMahon describes how the absence of consent by consultants for their patients to be included in the research project undermined not only the research project, but also the intentions of the funding agency. However, the extent to which that investigator could force the issue was limited by the possible detrimental effects for subsequent researchers and even the suspicion that it was possible that one or more individual consultants were waiting for him to overstep what might be judged as reasonable behaviour for a nurse researcher. It may be that some members of the medical profession may not take nurses working as researchers seriously, as Jane Robinson experienced. Thus Jane argues that the creation of knowledge is not sufficient in itself to bring about change in practice and that action research is the means to effect this change.

It would seem that the complexity of examining and using the politics of research is one of the unrecognized skills that researchers acquire from their early studies; it would be interesting to examine what proportion of a research student's time in discussion with his or her supervisor is spent on these issues.

Another recurring theme throughout the studies described in this book is that the stages of the research process employed by research textbooks and research courses are not as logical and ordered as they first appear. Whilst few would be naive enough to consider the research process to be like an escalator, where if one makes it onto the first step the end point is inevitably reached, there is a perception that there is a path that, with a little help, most investigators can navigate without mishap. Unfortunately, a number of the authors found the belief to be fallacious. In trying to define an area of enquiry under considerable constraints, Jane Miles experienced feelings of desperation when she went through a number of false starts and disappointments. It was only through reflection on her dilemmas that she developed creative solutions to her research problems.

Reflection on the researcher's own work and forming a

judgement about the adequacy, suitability and value of what has been done at each stage is a worthwhile exercise, requiring a stout heart. This is particularly well demonstrated in Alison Richardson's chapter (Chapter 5), in which she describes four phases of pilot work which she undertook in order to ensure that she had developed the most appropriate and effective tools for measuring the important variables associated with the self-care behaviours of patients with chemotherapy induced nausea. This repeated circling back in the same part of the research process was also the experience of Kath Ross (Chapter 9) who, through her experience of analysing qualitative data, again under time and other constraints, clearly demonstrates that research can be anything but a linear process. Ross's chapter also shows how there are certain situations where textbooks cannot help the researcher; instead the investigator must use his or her own creativity in order for the project to proceed.

The need for creativity in running even the simplest study is to some extent a result of the lack of agreement between the expectations of the researcher and the reality of the project. This theme recurs through many chapters, but may be found in Ann Bergen's work (Chapter 8), in which she describes how she deals with totally divergent findings from the two data collection methods that she employed in her study exploring experiences of terminal illness in the community. The challenge in making sense of, and presenting, contradictory data was dealt with by Ann remaining open and alert to possible reasons for such findings. Clearly, any attempt to hold fixed ideas about how the research should proceed from the beginning would have been fruitless. Instead, there is a need for researchers to remain alert, sensitive and flexible at all stages of the research process in order to identify the unique issues requiring attention and thus acknowledgement and implementation of change in each individual study. This may result in the creation of further work, as Richard (Chapter 6) found, or a delay in the research process, as Alison (Chapter 5) demonstrated, but the contribution to the knowledge of the subject concerned outweighs this.

The ability of the researcher to be reflective and creative is undoubtedly facilitated by expert supervision. Adequate and appropriate supervision ensures that not only are dilemmas

and decisions during the research process competently approached, but that the researcher learns from the experience,
applying or modifying, where possible, theory to practice.

CONCLUSION

Despite the fact that there are known to be problems in translating research findings into practice and the clear message
from this book that the research process is not an easy one, it is
likely that the interest in, and volume of, research in nursing
will continue to expand rapidly. The history of nursing research
is not very long and over the last 40 years it has broadly
developed from others performing research on nurses, through
nurses investigating themselves to nurses examining their
practice and how this influences our patients. There is now a
recognition that registered nurses at all levels should have an
understanding and appreciation of the research process. It is
our belief that the large number of research texts that have
accompanied this heightening of awareness have failed fully
to illuminate the experience of research. This book aims to
provide, through accounts of real research, the other side of
the story. This is becoming even more pertinent as nurses become increasingly aware that they do not need to have practised
research in order to value and understand it.

However, this problem solving is the real learning that is
achieved through performing research as a learning exercise as
part of an MSc or other course. The steps of the research process,
the advantages and disadvantages of different methodologies
and methods and the choice and performance of analysis can
all be taught, memorized and reproduced in essays and examinations. However, it is only by reflecting on the experience
of 'doing research' that the ability of the individual as a competent investigator can be effectively developed. We hope that
the experiences described in this book assist in the development
of nurse researchers, as well as increase awareness of the
research process among nurses.

The need to be aware of the politics of research and the
necessity of effectively addressing them to ensure that an appropriate, reliable and valid study takes place are graphically
described by the accounts in this book. Further, the research
process has been shown to be a messy and, at times, dis-

organized process, requiring creativity and reflection at all stages and that it is not the ordered linear process implied by many research texts.

We hope that through these accounts, which come from nurses with varying degrees of experience in performing research, a new contribution will be made to nursing knowledge which will assist in the development and selection of methodologies most appropriate for investigating nursing.

REFERENCES

Abraham, I.L., Schultz, S., Polis, N., Vines, S.W., and Smith, M.C. (1987) Research-on-research: the meta-analysis of nursing and health research, in *Research Methodology*, (ed. M.C. Cahoon), Churchill Livingstone, Edinburgh.

Bell, C. and Roberts, H. (1984) *Social Researching. Politics, Problems and Practice*, Routledge and Kegan Paul, London.

Burgess, R.G. (1984) *In the Field: An Introduction to Field Research*, George Allen & Unwin, London.

Ecock-Connelly, C. (1986) Replication research in nursing. *International Journal of Nursing Studies*, 23(1), 71–8.

Hockey, L. (1985) *Nursing Research: Mistakes and Misconceptions*, Churchill Livingstone, Edinburgh.

Hunt, M. (1987) The process of translating research findings into nursing practice. *Journal of Advanced Nursing*, 12, 101–10.

McMahon, R. (1991) The prevalence of skin problems beneath the breasts of in-patients. *Nursing Times (Occasional Paper)*, 87(39), 48–51.

Reed, J. and Robbins, I. (1991) Research rituals. *Nursing Times*, 87(23), 50–1.

Romney, M.L. (1982) Nursing research in obstetrics and gynaecology. *International Journal of Nursing Studies*, 19(4), 193–203.

2

Defining the research question

Jane Miles

INTRODUCTION

Defining the research question is arguably one of the most difficult stages of any research project because so much depends on it. When deciding upon the research question the researcher has to have an idea of what lies ahead – the approach, methods of data collection and the type of data analysis that is going to be used. As a result, it is not something that can be written easily but the development of a research question is a stage of any project that requires a lot of work. Unless the question is clear, concise and answerable then the study will not progress in a logical, scientific manner.

The following chapter describes my experiences of defining a research question in the context of a dissertation required for the second year of a two year MSc in Nursing. Cormack and Benson (1991) raise two important questions about this stage of the research process. These are 'How do I find a research question?' and 'How can I decide which question to study?'. It is the answers to these two questions which form the basis of this chapter.

GETTING STARTED

The first stage in formulating a research question is to identify a broad area of interest. Redfern (1984) says, 'Asking the research question involves a process of developing a vague hunch into a precise, unambiguous and researchable question'. However at this stage I didn't even have a vague hunch! Cormack and Benson (1991) suggest that research questions can be found via your own experience, professional literature, theoretical frameworks, conferences and study days or national directives and delphi studies. Often people do have ideas from their own professional practice that they feel highly motivated to look at. Many research books give the impression that there are so many thousands of questions to be asked in nursing practice that selecting one will be easy. For example, Clark (1987) says, 'Ideas for research are everywhere. We are constantly bombarded with sensible ideas that need to be explored'. However I do not remember being 'bombarded'. I could not identify one area of interest, let alone a question! I also remember feeling that all my colleagues on the course had a valid and straightforward plan of action but that I was so far behind because I didn't even have a question to ask. I understand from others that this is a common feeling. At this stage in the research process time seems to be of the essence. Getting started always seems to be the worst part especially as you become intensely aware that minutes and hours until the date of submission are ticking away.

I was desperate for an idea, any idea, so I began by asking around. Surely someone out there in practice would have an exciting question that they felt must be asked but not the knowledge or resources to pursue? Surely one of my colleagues would relieve my suffering by a quick phone call or an anonymous note put into my post signed by 'A Wellwisher?' In retrospect, even if they had, I expect that I would have lacked the motivation to produce a good piece of work based on their question, not mine. As Cormack and Benson (1991) state, 'Unless the research question focuses on a problem about which *you* feel strongly, it is likely that during difficult times you will be unable to sustain enthusiasm for the study'.

Again in retrospect there were many questions from my own practice in elderly care which I could have asked but I was so totally immersed in practice problems that I was having difficulty in seeing the wood for the trees and I needed to feel inspired by something new and exciting. One of the major factors which influenced this was that I was doing the research part time with a one day a week release from practice. I was often feeling tired on my study days so I felt that I needed to look at something totally new that would fire my enthusiasm. I

on's inability. Furthermore, due to the very individuality
ach person, the effect on a person of that inability will vary
that variation affects the problem as well as its solution.
each individual person presents the nurse with unique
lems. From this it follows that the solution to the problem
t be equally unique if it is to fully address the person's
lem, in that the solution will be based on the factors
ributing to the problem, the response of the individual and
he experience and expertise of the individual nurse. Thus
lem solving is not only inherent to nursing practice but
problem identification and problem solving in nursing is
ntially unique to each individual situation, although clearly
ng some elements of generalizability. The uniqueness of
situation clearly demands the artistry (creativity) to which
n refers.

f course whilst defining the research question I should
thought through what creativity had to do with nursing
logical way and should have been able to articulate this.
vever unless the researcher is highly experienced in re-
ch, i.e. post-doctoral, framing the research question or
ing for relationships will always be a developmental pro-
with increasing understanding of the topic. This develop-
tal process was not comfortable. Not only had I not got it
traight in my own mind but any idea takes a lot of living
before it can be articulated convincingly. Research on any
ract notion cannot be defended in one sentence because of
omplexity. Throughout the project I would try and defend
t would much rather have said, 'Just bear with me – it's
y important to nursing. If you can wait for the answer I'll
it to you when I've fully thought it through myself. I just
this burning hunch that it's very important!'

e sort of question going around in my head at this time was
nurses creative?' I must have felt disillusioned with nurs-
t this present time because my gut feeling was 'No!' or 'Not
y!'. This was reinforced by some of my reading. Bowman
) states that traditionally nursing has been routinized,
rchical and authority orientated. This pattern of organ-
on encourages individuals to become convergent thinkers
takes away their authority for decision making. Indeed
lmayr (1969) suggests that the domineering pattern of
ing attracts focused thinkers into the profession. Thus both

acknowledge that this is not everybody's experience. Indeed
many people would rather do something closely related to
their work so that they can feel immersed and can feed their
research into their practice.

IDENTIFYING AN AREA FOR QUESTIONING

When it became obvious that no one was going to present a
research question to me on a plate I began my search in earnest.
I read a lot and went through back copies of journals. I particularly chose the *Journal of Advanced Nursing* and the *International
Journal of Nursing Studies* to look through because these were
very general in their content, were academic in nature and
very often researchers would mention 'Implications for further
research' at the end of their paper. After leafing through several
journals I came across an article about creativity and nursing
(Jones, 1983).

This article sparked off an interest for several reasons. Firstly
I had always been interested in psychology, including psychological constructs and their application to nursing. Secondly I
was more interested in nurses and their actions as a potential
research topic than I was in patients for this particular study.
This was because I only had one academic year to develop the
proposal, collect the data, analyse the results and write up the
study. I knew that I could save time by using a sample of
nurses in the study, as access to this sample would be much
easier to achieve than any other. Also I would not be required
to submit my proposal to the ethics committee in the particular
health authority in which I would be conducting the study,
because at this time they only looked at studies involving
patients. This did not mean that my study did not raise any
ethical issues and indeed the majority of ethics committees
now want to see any proposal related to their health authority.
However not having to go to the ethics committee meant that
my plan of action could be totally dictated by my own pace of
work.

After reading the article by Jones (1983) I felt inspired to
consider this as a potential area for research as her review of
the literature highlighted the fact that little work had been
done on creativity in nursing. Also it suddenly dawned on me

how much the word 'creative' or 'creativity' was being used in nursing. For example a report by the DHSS (1988) stated that:

> Frequently such [nursing care] plans are based on the nursing process which is a method which encourages a problem solving, systematic, yet creative approach to care. This approach is one which we support . . .

Also several books were published with the word 'creative' in their titles, suggesting something good and innovative, e.g. Faulkner (1988). People talked about innovative and creative care in the same breath. Indeed creativity was mentioned in several educational objectives that I read, as well as job descriptions. It seemed to me that the problem identification and problem solving employed by the new type of practitioner described within Project 2000 (UKCC, 1986), who is said to be autonomous and independent, requires a high level of creativity. Therefore I came to believe creative nursing must in turn equal good nursing.

WHAT'S CREATIVITY GOT TO DO WITH NURSING?

At this stage it was important that I logically thought through why creativity was important in nursing. I was doing a Masters course in Nursing and therefore I fully expected to have to defend my reasoning. As the study progressed this expectation was justified. When people asked 'What are you doing for your research?' and I then informed them, the most frequent response was 'What's creativity got to do with nursing?'

I think that probably the first time I realized that creativity was an important concept to be explored was after I had gained a superficial knowledge of the works of Schon (1983) which I came across in other areas of my work. Subsequently Schon had a very significant influence on my work. However it is interesting to note that I came across his concepts accidentally and not through my systematic reading relating to creativity.

Schon stated that professional practice was often looked upon in terms of being the 'high hard ground'. The high ground consists of problems that can be solved by applying theory and looking for research evidence. However Schon points out that most of the problems in professional practice are in the 'swampy lowlands' because they are unique and often difficult to solve.

Nevertheless, inherent in all professionals v petent is a core of artistry that can deal v lowlands' by the 'art of problem framing, t tation and the art of improvisation'. Artistr an exercise of intelligence, a kind of kno that is demonstrated within the swampy l Therefore Schon sees the expert professi creating in practice:

> constantly observing, assessing, doing, tioning the observations, the judgement justing, questioning assumptions and l from another angle.

In reading more around the subject of cr how Schon's use and definition of artistry resemblance to certain definitions of crea Pesut (1985) stated that 'Creativity better produces a plan, or results in a pattern, : not clearly presented before'.

At this point it became fairly obvious problem solving went hand in hand. Hav link in my own mind I was able to see how nursing more clearly. Problem solving is aspect of nursing. Numerous theorists def concerned with assisting, in some way, in retain optimal health (e.g. Orem, 1980, an Further, most definitions of the nursing refer to problem solving (Brunner and Sudd 1985). In practice nursing activity can be increasingly to the problems with whic senting, e.g. problems of inability to main

Effective problem solving is only neces unique nature of problems as they are individual patient. If problems were gen dividual practitioner need not be a good example, if problem X was identified spec A, B and C, then it might be automaticall R, S and T. This, however, is not usually tl of being unable to dress oneself can be of reasons with one or several contributi the organization and the individuals within nursing might be seen to militate against independent practice.

REFINING THE RESEARCH QUESTION

If 'Are nurses creative?' was going to be my research question then it was important that firstly I defined what I meant by creativity and that secondly I decided how I was going to measure it. I soon discovered from the literature (e.g. Guildford, 1950) that it was the problems raised by these two areas that had led to creativity remaining a neglected area of study in all disciplines.

When an attempt has been made to define creativity it has usually been in terms of the product of the process or in terms of the process itself. The problem with defining creativity in terms of the product alone is that it does not take account of process issues such as human relationships. Tyson (1972) gives the example of a housewife and mother who may be creative in providing a happy and supportive background for her family. However, it is not possible to assess what appears to be intangible. Rogers (1954) defines creativity in terms of the process itself and it is his definition that I decided to use in this study. Rogers states that:

> The creative process is the emergence in action of a novel relational product, growing out of the uniqueness of the individual on the one hand, and the materials, events, people or circumstances of his life on the other. (p. 249)

In spite of the appropriateness of this definition to the nursing situation, translating it into appropriate measurement tools was somewhat problematic. I now know that I began the wrong way around. I started by looking at how nurses displayed their creativity or lack of it in practice, rather than saying 'How have experts measured creativity before?'. Initially I thought of analysing the care plans that nurses wrote as what was written on paper is purported to be a true representation of what goes on in practice. However I very quickly dismissed this idea as I knew from personal experience that what was written in these care plans did not necessarily reflect what was done in practice. Therefore if I retained my interest in the nurses' ability to creatively problem solve rather than its demonstration in practice I would have to look at their problem solving in some other way. One option would have been to set up some sort of problem in practice and then observe what the nurses did and how they dealt with the problem. However I knew that this would not be practical and I would have to settle for setting them some problems about nursing practice to solve on paper.

I did recognize that there would be severe limitations in terms of whether any of the research tools measured what they were supposed to measure. There was also no indication that the respondents' theoretical replies on paper would reflect their practical activities. Bearing in mind Bendall's (1975) findings that there was a 63% non-correlation between what students said they would do in examinations and what they actually did do in practice, it seems highly unlikely!

The next hurdle that had to be crossed was that even if I did set problems for nurses to solve then in what way was I going to analyse the data? This was the point at which I came nearest to abandoning the whole idea of trying to explore such an abstract concept. It was my supervisor who stated the obvious. I had already identified that there was no widely accepted theory of creativity which would direct efforts at specifying an adequate assessment procedure; neither was there any one widely accepted theory of problem solving. However I would have to use some already established creativity tests as well as setting situations that could be construed as problems for the respondents to sort out. The purpose of using these tests in the study was so that they could serve as a baseline against which nurses' solutions to problems could be examined.

By now I was beginning to feel that the whole project was quite possible. What I was overlooking was the fact that I had to obtain some creativity tests that were quite straightforward and guidelines as to how to analyse them. I also had to think up some practice situations which didn't require particularly specialized knowledge and to which all nurses could relate.

Finding the creativity tests was quite straightforward. There were many examples available in various books. However, what was not so easy to find was information on what to do with the responses and how they were to be scored. I ended up using three of Torrance's (1966) Minnesota Tests of Creative Thinking because the instructions for using them were very clear and concise and guidelines for the analysis could be found although these were a bit vague in some respects. Another reason for choosing these creativity tests was that Torrance has indicated his concern for problem solving in his definition of creative thinking. He states that creative thinking is:

> the process of sensing gaps or disturbing, missing elements; testing these hypotheses; and communicating the results, possibly modifying and retesting the hypotheses.
>
> (*Torrance, 1962*)

Three tests were chosen from the Minnesota Tests of Creative Thinking because they were so different from one another and could therefore be assumed to be testing either different aspects of creativity or creativity expressed in different ways.

In searching the literature on creativity I found that the use of the creativity tests mentioned above left two main questions unanswered.

1. Do the predictive instruments measure variables directly related to creativity? It may be possible to distinguish the subjects but for the wrong reason. For example, it could be argued that the above tests would prove an ability to think but would not necessarily prove that an individual is creative.
2. Are the tests valid even though they do not establish a correlation with practical criteria? For example, if a nurse is good at giving multiple answers to the above tests, does this ability correlate with creativity in terms of problem solving or practice?

As mentioned previously I did try and anticipate this by developing some situations in and out of practice that could be construed as problems. This was not at all easy as it required some creativity on my part!

THE COMPONENTS OF THE RESEARCH QUESTION

Prior to reading extensively I had thought that I had established what my research question was going to be – 'Are nurses creative?' I was now not at all sure that it was an answerable question. I had made the mistake that many inexperienced researchers make and that was to try and do too much. Attempting to show that nurses were not very creative seemed to be the nub of the question to me but it was in fact something much simpler – 'Can creative problem solving in nurses be identified?'

In order to get to such a seemingly simple question I had already unearthed many complexities. By now I knew that there were many components to this research question. These differing components of the one question were expressed as the following aims.

1. To identify possible tools to measure creative problem solving in nurses.

Within this aim I hoped to explore the reliability and validity of the established creativity tests with my sample. I also hoped to see if I could analyse some nursing and non-nursing situations using the indicators suggested by the Minnesota Tests of Creative Thinking (fluency, flexibility, originality and elaboration). Not only was I interested in whether nurses were able to problem solve but I was also interested in the reasons for the solutions that they gave. Therefore linked with the problem situations was a questionnaire which was given to each respondent after they had answered the question on each situation. This instrument was used because it was considered important to see whether the respondents were overtly basing their answers on past experience and whether they saw that there were any constraints to the way in which they problem solved in their environment.

2. To examine the influence of the variables of work environment, education and training, previous experience, age and sex on creativity and problem solving.

I chose to examine the influence of these variables for several reasons. Firstly the literature search had indicated that there was a link between creativity and several of these variables. Secondly my professional experience led me to believe that there may be a link. For example, there seemed to be a belief at practice level that the primary nursing role was one that required nurses to be creative. Thirdly I had decided to use a convenience sample of nurses who were on courses, study days or workshops held in one health authority. Collecting the data from a sample that were brought together in small groups would reduce the possiblity of contamination of data although it did not eradicate it entirely. In making these decisions about the sample it became obvious that the creative abilities of this group were liable to be influenced by a very broad range of variables, e.g. work environment, education and training, etc.

3. To examine the relationship between creativity scores of differing tests, problem solving in differing situations and between creativity scores and problem solving.

This third and final aim was developed because the validity of the nursing and non-nursing situations had to be established. Also the validity of the creativity tests in establishing any practical criteria to do with nursing, even though on paper, had to be examined.

CONCLUSIONS

Cormack and Benson (1991) state that 'The process of asking the research question is, in part, simply the logical application of a number of guidelines'. However even if I had known that there were any guidelines, or indeed how to apply them, I doubt that it would have helped. I began formulating a research question by identifying a broad area of interest. I did this by looking through the literature. At the same time I identified the sort of study that I was interested in doing and the constraints that were upon me. The factors that influenced my decision were to do with my interest and motivation and the resources that were available to me. The time that I had available was also important and wrapped up with this was some knowledge that I had about the ethics committee and the sort of studies that they wanted to see. However the most influential factor concerning the time available was that the whole project had to be done in the space of one academic year. Decisions made about my sample followed from this, i.e. that they were nurses in one health authority.

I also had to think through what creativity had to do with nursing. I know that in theory I should have done this before I began the project. However in reality the whole developmental process improves with researcher expertise. At the same time I had to identify how creativity presented itself in professional practice. If I had not been able to identify this, then I would not have been able to proceed with the project. At the outset I had thought that the question that I was going to ask was 'Are nurses creative?' However I soon found that this was not a researchable question and that I had fallen into the trap of trying to do too much. Again, this is something often done by inexperienced researchers. Nevertheless when I realized that there were so many difficulties, particularly with the definition of creativity and its measurement, then the research question was refined further to become 'Can creative problem solving in nurses be identified?'

The main lesson that I learned from this experience of formulating a research question was that there is not a particular procedure to follow but that quite often it is a journey of discovery and indeed a problem solving exercise in itself. The problems that arise in nursing research are many and varied. These problems are unique and require unique solutions, albeit solutions that may have generalized knowledge as their base. This type of problem identification and problem solving could be argued to require a high level of creativity!

REFERENCES

Aichlmayr, R.H. (1969) Creative nursing. *Journal of Nurse Education*, **8**.
Bendall, E. (1975) *So, You Passed, Nurse*, Royal College of Nursing, London.
Bowman, M.P. (1986) *Nursing Management and Education: A Conceptual Approach to Change*, Croom Helm, London.
Brunner, L.S. and Suddarth, D.S. (1980) *Medical–Surgical Nursing*, Lippincott, Philadelphia.
Champion, R. (1988) *Competent Nurse? Reflective Practitioner?* Paper given at the 1st International Conference on Nurse Education, Cardiff.
Cormack, D.F.S. and Benson, D.C. (1991) Asking the research question, in *The Research Process in Nursing*, 2nd edn, (ed. D.F.S. Cormack), Blackwell Scientific, London.
DHSS (1988) Letter from Chief Nursing Officer, ref. PL/CNO (88)17.
Faulkner, A. (1985) *Nursing – A Creative Approach*, Baillière Tindall, London.
Guilford, J.P. (1950) Creativity. *American Psychologist*, **5**, 444–54.
Henderson, V. (1960) *Basic Principles of Nursing Care*, International Council of Nurses, London.
Jones, J.A. (1983) Where angels fear to tread – nursing and the concept of creativity. *Journal of Advanced Nursing*, **8**, 405–11.
Orem, D. (1980) *Nursing: Concepts of Practice*, McGraw Hill, New York.

Pesut, D.J. (1985) Toward a new definition of creativity. *Nurse Educator*, **10**(1), 5.

Redfern, S. (1984) Asking the research question, in *The Research Process in Nursing*, 1st edn, (ed. D.F.S. Cormack), Blackwell Scientific, London.

Rogers, C. (1954) Toward a theory of creativity. *ETC: A Review of General Semantics*, **11**, 249–60.

Schon, D.A. (1983) *The Reflective Practitioner: How Professionals Think in Action*, Temple Smith, London.

Torrance, E.P. (1962) *Role of Evaluation in Creative Thinking*. Report on Project No. 725, Cooperative Research Bureau, University of Minnesota.

Torrance, E.P. (1966) *Torrance Tests of Creative Thinking: Norms and Technical Manual*, Personnel Press, Priceton.

Tyson, M. (1972) Creativity in new horizons, in *Psychology*, (ed. B.M. Foss), Pelican, Harmondsworth.

UKCC (1986) *A New Preparation for Practice – Project 2000*, UKCC, London.

3

Choosing an appropriate methodology

Judith Lathlean

INTRODUCTION

Deciding on the overall research approach is sometimes felt to be a relatively straightforward procedure, especially by the novice researcher. Initial comments such as 'I'll just do a survey to find out what the patients think about primary nursing', or 'What we need here is an experiment to test out which treatment works best' are not uncommon. The reality, however, is far more complex and it is often not possible to choose a methodology before many other aspects have been taken into consideration.

This chapter highlights the kind of issues that are faced, both in making an initial decision about the methodology or research design and in the development of the design during the research project. It is based primarily on my experiences of undertaking one particular project – an evaluation of an innovative training scheme for ward sisters (Lathlean and Farnish, 1984) – but I will also touch upon my current concerns in relation to an ongoing study of lecturer practitioners in nursing. These projects have been chosen for a number of reasons, but especially because they illustrate two major concerns in research: the use of a methodology that is not as widely employed and as well understood as some and the necessity to review, to refine and even to be prepared to change the research design.

A BRIEF FOR A RESEARCH PROJECT

The outline – provided by the funding bodies – for the first project indicated that 'an evaluation of an experimental training scheme for ward sisters using an action research strategy' was required. Nevertheless, it was important for me not to take it at its face value and, as a reasonably experienced researcher when appointed to do the research, I was used to making up my own mind about the methodology to be adopted for my projects.

I needed to consider carefully why it was thought that an action research approach should be used. Was it because the funders of the research had decided, like Greenwood (1984), that 'action research is the most appropriate research strategy in nursing' and should therefore be the automatic design of choice? Or maybe it was because they adhered to a particular philosophy of research? There are those, for example, who argue that action research epitomizes a preferred alternative philosophical approach to the study of society and its problems. Some contrast it with a positivist philosophy, 'which considers scientific knowledge only to be obtainable from sense data that can be directly experienced and verified' (Susman and Evered, 1978) and which stresses the possibility of an 'objective' reality. Others promote action research as a third alternative – that is, a 'critical science' research approach – to remedy the weaknesses of both a positivist and an interpretive view of social sciences (for example, Carr and Kemmis, 1986, and Webb, 1989). If one is persuaded that research in a particular style, or using a certain philosophical paradigm, is all-important then this will tend to dictate the research strategy employed.

On the other hand, action research may have been suggested as a way of avoiding a lengthy evaluative research project which reached conclusions either too late or with too little time to implement them, since it offers the opportunity to combine research with action and improvement as the project proceeds. At the outset of the project, I was unsure which – if any – of these views influenced the statement that action research was to be used! Further, maybe the reasoning behind the expressed desire for action research was at fault. Indeed, was it the best, the most appropriate or even a viable strategy, given the aims of the project?

In order to answer these questions and to make firm decisions about our research design, my research colleague and I – together we formed the research team – needed to do a number of things. First, and perhaps most importantly, we had to consider the aims of the research and the questions to be addressed by the project. Second, we had to think about such issues as the kind of explanation, generalization and understanding that was both desirable and possible. And third, we had to decide whether we were going to adopt an interventionist stance or try to remain outside the phenomena that we were trying to study. Needless to say, all these points are interrelated. So, for example, the research aim should guide us on whether we should be 'internal' or 'external' to the research and the research questions should throw some light on our views about generalization and explanation.

How we decided on our research design will be elaborated shortly, but first an outline of the project and its evaluation is given. Also, it is important to put decisions about methodology in the context of a vital concurrent activity – that of looking carefully at the literature, in this instance, especially on action research.

THE WARD SISTER TRAINING PROJECT

In the late 1970s, the King Edward's Hospital Fund for London set up an experimental scheme for the training of ward sisters in two hospitals for a limited period of up to five years. The scheme was based on certain premises: the need for specific ward-based training for ward sisters, the appropriateness of a joint education and service approach and the importance of role modelling as a major method of teaching and learning about the job of a sister.

The scheme focused on two 'training' wards – one in a London teaching hospital and the other in a non-teaching hospital – and it had specially appointed personnel for each ward, a tutor and a ward sister who were known as 'preceptors'. They were jointly responsible for the development of the curriculum and for the teaching of the ward sister trainees (usually newly appointed sisters in their first ward sister post) either in or near the training wards for three months and then for the support of trainees back in their own wards for a further three months. (Details of the scheme can be found in Allen, 1982, and King's Fund, 1982.)

It was felt that the scheme should be evaluated, initially for a period of three years, and thus a project was established with joint funding from the King's Fund and the Department of Health and Social Security within the Nursing Education Research Unit of Chelsea College.

The literature on action research

I had been appointed to lead the project, presumably because of my relevant previous research experience and because I had convinced the panel that I knew about action research. However, it was only when I started delving into the literature that I realized how naïve was my understanding. I had this rather hazy notion – shared by many others at the time – that action research was a label given to a situation whereby if you attempted to put into practice research findings, that is, if there was any combination of research and action, then you were in effect conducting action research!

The literature review served not only to confirm my ignorance about the strategy but also, at least initially, to confuse. At the time of the study many of the standard research texts in nursing did not even mention it as a possible research strategy. Further, there seemed to be very few examples of action research in nursing and the ones that could be found, such as Tierney (1973), which was described as a combined experimental and action study, and Towell and Harries (1979), which involved the facilitation of change within a psychiatric hospital, seemed to exhibit quite different characteristics.

It was necessary in the main, therefore, to turn to literature from outside nursing, especially that of organizational development and education. From this it was apparent that action research was first proposed as a way of applying understanding generated from the social sciences to the solution of social problems, that it was either quite large scale and long term in nature or it related to specific situations, that it was usually collaborative with an inter-relationship between the researchers and the practitioners, and that the processes followed could often be described as cyclical or forming a spiral towards the attainment of a known goal.

What became apparent from the reading, though not until we were well into the project, was the lack of agreement amongst commentators as to what were the *essential* features of action research. This contrasts strongly with an experimental methodology where there is considerable agreement about the correct principles and procedures. Thus, whereas some say that action research is about solving problems in a specific setting (Cohen and Manion, 1980), it does not necessarily always involve a 'problem'. Neither is it invariably collaborative – some is conducted by practitioners acting as researchers and examining the effectiveness of their own practice. Nor is it always cyclical, since it is possible to proceed in a linear way, moving from A to B to C and so on towards the achievement of a goal. However, in considering the examples of action research, three main features appear to be distinctive. First, action research is about taking action in the real world and a close examination of the effects of the action taken; thus it always involves intervention. Second, it is located within a specific situation and takes account of the context; and third, the ability to generalize the findings is tentative and by the use of social science theory rather than probability theory, as in experiments and surveys.

The research aims and questions as a starting point

There are many reasons why particular approaches to research are chosen, but since research is about satisfying research aims and about asking and answering questions, a good starting point for making such a decision is to consider the aims and the *nature* of the research questions to be addressed.

The aims of our study were given in an early unpublished paper as 'helping to i) define a model of ward sister training, and ii) define the effect on the ward environment and patient care'. However, on further investigation, it became evident that the research team was not in a position to 'define' a model of ward sister training but rather 'to examine in detail a given model . . . to assess the effects of the scheme, and to assist in the modification of the scheme in order to achieve a practical method of training ward sisters' (Lathlean and Farnish, 1984). The first two parts of this aim – the examination of a particular scheme and the assessment of outcomes – would imply the use of an evaluative case study approach, but the latter aspect of facilitating the development of the innovation seemed to mean the use of action research.

We were happy about the first implication. Nevertheless, we were slightly nervous at the prospect of the second. For a start, the scheme did not equate to a 'problem' needing to be solved, unless the problem was viewed as the general one of ward sisters lacking preparation for their roles and the 'solution' as the implementation of a scheme aimed at their better preparation. And second, to what extent would participants in the scheme welcome or even accept our role in improving it? However, our first concern was addressed by the realization that not all action research sets out to solve problems, but rather to develop. The second was more a matter of the reality of conducting the research rather than the appropriateness of the methodology, though of course, if our research design was dependent upon the involvement of others who were not prepared to collaborate, this would make our task difficult if not impossible.

From the overall aims of the research, we developed a number of initial research questions that we hoped would be tackled by the research. These were various, but covered three main areas of interest. Examples only of research questions are given.

The process of change

What are the processes through which the scheme is institutionalized within the two hospitals? What strategies facilitate this process?

The training of ward sisters

How do trainees learn the role of ward sister? What are the contributions of different training arrangements to this process?

The role of the ward sister

What is the role of ward sister in this scheme? How does this role compare with the generally accepted view of the ward sister role?

Then as the scheme and the research progressed, we had another area of interest.

The modification of the scheme

How can aspects of the scheme, especially those deemed problematic, be modified and changed so as to meet the aims and objectives of the scheme?

In line with the research aims, these illustrative research questions pointed the way to a phased research design with different elements and again, the type of questions relating to the first three areas suggested in the main an indepth case study approach, whereas the fourth area indicated an action research strategy.

Explanation, understanding and generalization

Though pointing in a definite direction, the research questions in themselves were not sufficient determinants of the research design. We were also interested in the kind of *explanation* to be achieved by the research. One powerful research tradition views explanation in terms of events being related in time. This is very much the logic of experimental research, where you are trying to demonstrate that two (or more) 'variables' are causally related in that one tends to give rise to or alternatively to be caused by the other. It could be argued that we were interested in the relationship between variables, such as the inputs to and outcomes of the scheme, but we were not only concerned with whether things were related but the mechanism by which they were connected. So, for example, we wanted to know about the processes and strategies which appeared to lead to successful or conversely to less effective outcomes. Therefore, we needed a research design that not only indicated whether things appeared to be related but how they were related.

We also needed to ask the question, 'To what extent do we want to *understand* people and their activities?'. Historically much research in nursing has been about describing people in terms of imposed categories and from a so-called 'objective' and external viewpoint. This gives some kind of understanding, but unless the researcher tries to see the world or the specific context through someone else's eyes, to gain access to the sense they make of their situation, then they will be limited in their understanding of them.

Therefore, we had to consider whether it was appropriate or possible for us to provide or impose categories and fit the data to these within a theoretical framework determined by us, or whether we wanted to try to see the situation as others saw it in terms of the concepts and terms they used, the logic of their actions and so on. In our study, we did not know sufficiently what our 'categories' would be, especially at the outset, and certainly we wanted to understand the experience of the scheme from the perspectives of those involved in it. This immediately meant that certain research approaches – namely case study and action research – were preferable.

In research we are always interested in the extent to which the findings are applicable more widely than the setting under study. The *generalizability* of the research can be defined as:

> the degree to which the research procedures justify the inference that the findings represent something beyond the specific observations upon which they are based; in particular, the inference that the findings can be generalized from the sample to the entire target population
>
> (*Polit and Hungler, 1989*)

The reality is that we are often under pressure to claim a wide generalizability for our conclusions, otherwise the research might be seen to be trivial. Some, especially those of a 'positivist' persuasion, argue that there is no point in doing research unless we can justify making – in a very specific way – wider claims about the world at large from our research within a part of it.

In this respect, the classic tradition in research is to look for a certain kind of generalization, by the use of particular techniques. The research is designed around certain principles such as the notions of population and random sampling, so that the findings from the sample can be generalized to the population by means of probability theory or the use of statistical analysis.

We, however, were not in a position to do that since we were focusing on the particular – a training scheme with two designated wards and participants who were non-randomly selected. Our setting was idiosyncratic and, therefore, we could not claim (statistically) that findings from it necessarily would have relevance to other individuals, situations and settings. Nevertheless, we could describe the situation in such a way that allowed our 'audience' to recognize its wider applicability. Elliott and Ebbutt (1983) refer to this process as 'external validation' and suggest that 'The responsibility for externally validating the study lies with the user and not with the researcher'. Further, we could attempt to abstract concepts or to 'theorize' about our situation from our findings. This kind of more tentative generalization – by exposure of the findings to others to make judgements as to their applicability and by the development of theories that can be applied or 'tested out' elsewhere or at a further stage in the project – is typical of case study and action research.

The research strategy

Our final consideration at an early stage in the project was to do with the nature of our roles in the research. Were we wanting to remain outside the phenomena that we were studying or did we want to be part of or influence the situation? At the time I was a little uncertain, as it seemed that we wanted to do both – to first understand the many facets of the scheme without unduly affecting them and then in the 'action' phase, to play a much more active role in changing and modifying aspects.

Taking into account all the foregoing points about the type of research questions and our views on understanding, explanation, generalization and the role of the researchers, we started the project by undertaking an indepth study of many facets of the scheme. It was then only after some time that we made recommendations for change and modification to parts of it and, in conjunction with the participants, encouraged certain actions to be taken and changes to be made. Thus, with hindsight, we went from an increasingly focused case study approach into action research, though I did not make this distinction at the time. Rather we talked about progressing from an 'orientation' phase to 'monitoring' phases, with 'cycles of action' forming an integral aspect of the latter.

Since this project, I have found it useful to think of four different general approaches to research – those of experiment,

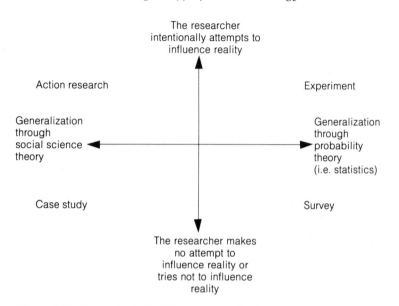

Figure 3.1 The context of different research strategies.

survey, case study and action research. Two of the important characteristics that distinguish these approaches are:

- the extent to which the real world is intentionally influenced in the research design, and
- the body of theory that is used to inform the research and generalize the findings – social science theory or probability theory.

If they are placed on two axes to form a matrix, the strategies can be plotted (Figure 3.1). So, for example, experimental research is characterized by the researcher influencing reality and by the ability to generalize the findings using probability theory, whereas conversely, with a case study, the researcher tries not to intervene and the findings are generalized tentatively by the use of theories derived from the social sciences. Had I been clearer about this kind of distinction when engaged in the project, I probably would have been less tentative about what to call our research design and more confident about the component parts of it!

Adhering to the research design

Descriptions of projects when the research is completed can give the impression that, once the design is set, it is a straightforward process to adhere to it or if deviations are presented, that they have been part of the original plan. This is far from so. There are many challenges to the methodology, both from within the project and from outside, that may necessitate responses ranging from a determination to stand firm come what may, to a complete revision of the design.

The ward sister project was no exception. On the one hand, there are concerns intrinsic to the research itself. First, there is the issue of moving from one 'phase' of the project to another when the phases are not distinct and obvious. For example, the literature on evaluation and case studies refers to becoming 'progressively more focused', but it was difficult for us to decide when our broad brush study of as many aspects of the scheme as possible should stop and how we should make decisions about the parts we would focus on. Also, it was never absolutely clear to us when we should move from the case study into the action research.

Second, there is the issue about what is the 'proper' way of going about the project. In experiments and surveys there are more clearcut procedures to follow and even if they prove difficult in practice, at least one knows the steps to be taking. However, certainly with action research and to some extent with case studies, at the time of our project there were few accounts of how to actually conduct such research and how to cope with the problems encountered.

Added to this, we had a fairly narrow view of what action research was and we were determined to pursue certain features we deemed essential, such as the seemingly straightforward 'cycles' of identification of the need for change, action, reflection and further change. Nevertheless, the process was by no means easy, nor did it follow the expected pattern. Also, what were the parameters of an action research cycle? Should we treat the whole project as one cycle or was it more appropriate to look at a number of mini-cycles within the whole, with different kinds of action proceeding at different speeds?

Third, in action research there is the problem of the role of the researchers in the action element. For example, some of the action in our project seemed to be happening of its own accord. Other facets – such as making changes to the content and presentation of the curriculum – appeared to be 'owned' by the participants in the scheme and we had little involvement, whereas further aspects, such as a review of the role of the preceptors and changes in the nature and organization of the ward experience for the trainees, were much more the result of collaboration between us and the practitioners, with the researchers feeding in their data and facilitating joint decision making with practitioners.

On the other hand, there can be pressures from outside the project. These may be to do with funding agencies requiring 'answers' in a certain space of time or being unhappy at the prospect of 'negative' findings. The main one for us was the reaction of others to our methodology. There were those who found it difficult to accept action research as a proper strategy. So for example, we were asked what theory we were proposing to test. We replied that we were trying to derive theoretical knowledge, rather than testing a theory. We were then challenged on having no control group to match against the experimental scheme. But, we argued, control is often intrinsic to action research in that one is trying to compare the relationship between our present system and the new (hopefully improved) system that we are setting up. Also, we were asked how we could hope to measure outcomes if we, in collaboration with others, were changing the inputs. We replied that it is in the nature of action research that the researcher takes action and that one is trying to ascertain the effectiveness of the action in achieving the desired change. Therefore the action researcher is just as interested in the *process* that was found necessary to achieve change as in the outcome that was gained, and the research is set up in such a way that it is possible to examine both process and outcomes.

There are still those who remain unconvinced that action research is indeed research at all and certainly, as we found, it is very difficult to sustain a good action research project. As a design, it is definitely not to be recommended for those who prefer neatness, precision and clear procedures to follow since it tends to be characterized by uncertainty, untidiness and an ongoing and continuous nature. Nevertheless, it is a challenging approach and, as mentioned before, a preferred strategy by some for understanding issues within nursing.

STUDYING LECTURER PRACTITIONERS

It was with this background and the experience of another action research project plus several shorter evaluative research projects that I embarked on a study of the developing roles of lecturer practitioners in one health authority. My natural inclination was towards action research – despite all the problems I had encountered in the past – or an evaluative approach. However, I ruled out action research at the outset on the grounds that whilst I wanted to study roles that in themselves were changing, I did not wish to contribute to or influence that change myself. My mode was to be essentially non-interventionist!

Nevertheless, I initially proceeded with the notion of evaluation, considering that my purpose was to ascertain the effectiveness of lecturer practitioners in reaching the aims and objectives set for them by the organization and generated by themselves. But after considerable preliminary work in refining my aims and developing my research questions, I considered that it was not possible to make judgements until I had a thorough understanding of the phenomena that I was interested in. And, since lecturer practitioners were new roles and the exploratory work indicated that they were by no means all likely to operate in the same way with, for example, different models of the role being put into practice, it seemed that I should concentrate on understanding what lecturer practitioners were, taking into account the different models, their relationship to their context and the wider implications for nurse education of the lecturer practitioner concept in action.

Developing and refining a methodology

Since the research questions were about the nature and reality of the job and I had certain views about the explanation, understanding and generalization I was seeking, a case study approach was indicated. The initial plan – prior to the first lecturer practitioners being appointed – was to study ten what I termed 'first generation' lecturer practitioners in depth for a period of time and then, when the role had become more stable, to study a much larger sample of 'second generation' ones, still using case study methodology. This plan was changed, in part for pragmatic reasons – it was quite some time before people were appointed to the posts and it would have taken too long to gain as many as ten in my first phase – but mainly because the five I recruited for the study were moving through a number of important and different phases in their development that I would have missed had I attempted to move on to a larger sample. Also by the end of the first period of fieldwork, I had by no means thoroughly answered my research questions.

Therefore the main aspect of my research – an ethnographic study of a small number of lecturer practitioners – was undertaken both on a smaller number than originally envisaged and over a very much longer period of time – almost three years instead of about one. Further, as I collected the data, the need to have separate phases for the project became clearer. Thus three emerged, each with its own clear rationale and relationship to the previous phase.

It was only when the research was well progressed – in the second phase – that certain key issues became strongly evident within the ethnography. These then formed the focus for the third phase of the ethnography. They are also the basis for two other parts of the study that it was decided to have – a study of the perspectives of people other than the lecturer practitioners (e.g. mentors, students, managers and lecturers) on the key issues, and a survey of all lecturer practitioners to see the extent to which the findings from the case studies can be generalized more widely to the much larger group of about 60 lecturer practitioners.

Experience now of several of these kinds of projects has convinced me that it is not only impossible to have an initial research design which is adhered to throughout, but also inappropriate to do so. In this study, the initial research questions were amenable to an ethnographic case study, but this has a particular logic which emphasizes the informants' perspective of their own practice, rather than the theoretical concerns of the researcher. The ethnography, the study of the plans and the literature review raised important issues about the lecturer practitioner role: for example, how viable is it, is the role as initially conceived, and to what extent is it directed towards resolving the endemic theory practice problems in nurse education as originally envisaged? Questions like these need to be explored other than through the ethnographic case study, but it is not until data have emerged from the latter that one would be in a position to decide what would be the appropriate means of addressing such questions.

CONCLUSION

The methodology that one chooses for a piece of research can be influenced by such wide ranging factors as personal inclination, the requirements and orientations of funding agencies and those in a position of power in relation to research, and a particular philosophical viewpoint about the nature of knowledge and the type of research that is preferred within a discipline such as nursing. Nevertheless, this chapter has sought to show that key considerations in the process must be the nature of the research questions and the type of explanation, understanding and the generalizability that one seeks. Nevertheless, in nursing research, the process of deciding on a research design is both difficult and complex and, whilst lessons can be learnt from each project undertaken, even the experienced researcher has to consider each project as a fresh challenge.

REFERENCES

Allen, H.O. (ed.) (1982) *The Ward Sister: Role and Preparation*, Baillière Tindall, London.
Carr, W. and Kemmis, S. (1986) *Becoming Critical: Education, Knowledge and Action Research*, The Falmer Press, Lewes.
Cohen, L. and Manion, L. (1980) *Research Methods in Education*, Routledge, London.
Elliott, J. and Ebbutt, D. (1983) *Action Research into Teaching for Understanding: A Guide to the TIQL Project*, Schools Council Publications, Longman, London.
Greenwood, J. (1984) Nursing research: a position paper. *Journal of Advanced Nursing*, **9**, 77–82.
King Edward's Hospital Fund for London (1982) *Ward Sister Preparation: A Contribution to Curriculum Building*, Project Paper No. 36, King's Fund, London.

Lathlean, J. and Farnish, S. (1984) *The Ward Sister Training Project: An Evaluation of a Training Scheme for Ward Sisters*, NERU Report No. 3, Chelsea College, University of London: Nursing Education Research Unit, London.

Polit, D. and Hungler, B. (1989) *Essentials of Nursing Research: Methods, Appraisal and Utilization*, 2nd edn, Lippincott, Philadelphia.

Susman, G. and Evered, R. (1978) An assessment of the scientific merits of action research. *Administrative Science Quarterly*, **23**, 582–603.

Tierney, A. (1973) Toilet training. *Nursing Times*, **69**, 1740–5.

Towell, D. and Harries, C. (eds) (1979) *Innovation in Patient Care: An Action Research Study of Change in a Psychiatric Hospital*, Croom Helm, London.

Webb, C. (1989) Action research: philosophy, methods and personal experiences. *Journal of Advanced Nursing*, **14**, 403–10.

4

People with AIDS: finding and accessing a hidden sample

Ken Nolan

INTRODUCTION

The process of selecting subjects or participants in a research project is directed by rules and guidelines set out in numerous research textbooks. However, like any stage of the research process sampling can be problematic. Researchers, be they nurses or students of other academic disciplines, acknowledge both the rules and guidelines and the problematic nature of sampling in planning and designing their studies. Despite meticulous planning sampling can and does go wrong. Whilst researchers know who and how they wish to select participants the realities of obtaining access to respondents, in the numbers required and from the desired background, can be very difficult. This chapter looks at the realities of sampling. In particular, it looks at the problems associated in accessing and sampling a hidden and vulnerable group, namely people with AIDS (acquired immune deficiency syndrome) and HIV (human immunodeficiency virus).

Herein lies the first issue in sampling potentially difficult groups: why conduct research into such problematic areas and groups? The glib answer would be, 'Why not?'. However, Stacey (1969) offers a rationale for such work. There is a need, she suggests, for research 'which honestly set(s) out to increase our knowledge of the facts of social life or to the furthering of our understanding of social relations'. AIDS is but one area of patient interaction and relationships where knowledge and understanding are poor.

This chapter also illustrates some of the difficulties and constraints of conducting sociological research related to people with AIDS (PWAs). In turn, it highlights the need for creativity, reflexivity and persistence in accessing and sampling such groups.

Although PWAs are in many ways a special case, nurse researchers face similar difficulties with other patient/client groups. Feldman and Johnson (1986) describe AIDS research as 'pioneering'. Whilst they refer to the formidable challenge faced by researchers in this new and difficult area, especially in the social sciences, the same can be said for nursing research per se. Much of what nurses research is new. Like any groups of researchers, nurses should not be daunted by these problems.

In order to explore the issues relating to sampling and accessing hidden groups it is necessary to start by putting the study into a social context.

BACKGROUND

AIDS cannot be viewed as another viral illness or fatal disease. What separates AIDS from other illnesses are the social actions which surround it and the groups which it affects. The spread of HIV and the development of AIDS in Europe and North America have been synonymous with homosexual behaviour, intravenous drug abuse and prostitution. The association of this fatal disease with groups who are marginalized and stigmatized by society has given rise to a complex range of social relations and problems. Nowhere, it would appear, are these relations more complex or problematic than in the area of health care.

Throughout the late 1970s and 1980s a moral panic ensued in response to the advent of AIDS. People with HIV/AIDS were seen as 'folk devils', responsible for all the moral ills of the day. The result of this 'scapegoating' was discrimination. Reports of those affected losing their homes and jobs or being refused essential services such as health care were commonplace. As with all moral panics the media, especially the press, played an active part in its development. Of interest to me were the reports of fellow health care workers (HCWs) refusing to care for, treat, touch or transport AIDS patients.

Surely this could not be so. Could individuals concerned with the care and well-being of others respond in such a negative way? This I assumed to be the wild fantasies of the tabloid press and yet another example of gutter journalism but a literature search revealed little evidence to refute the allegations made in the press. On the contrary, what little evidence there was suggested that such reports had some foundation. What clearly emerged was that there was a paucity of British social science research which explained the patients' interface with health care.

The research question began to emerge. My own research (Nolan, 1988) was aimed therefore at identifying the nature and patterns of interaction of PWAs with the health care system. It was necessary to know whether or not PWAs (this includes people with HIV, for society did not at the time differentiate between the two) did experience such a response from the health care system. Also, if they did, why were HCWs responding in such a manner?

OVERVIEW OF THE STUDY

Given this negative social response and the response of those affected, which was not to be visible to society, the problems for conducting research into the subject become obvious. Thus, the skill of the researcher is to design a study which is flexible and responsive to such issues and able to reach the target population whilst being valid and reliable. The discipline in which the research was conducted had the answers. The study sought not to prove or test a specific theory. Instead, it sought to generate theory by using interpretive methods and perspectives. In keeping with this perspective attempts were made to generate substantive grounded theory to explain the phenomenon. This method of theory development is described by its advocates as '. . . the discovery of theory from data – systematically obtained and analysed in social research . . .' (Glaser and Strauss, 1967).

These perspectives and their respective methods and methodologies are important for two reasons. Firstly there are implications for the methods used which should be reflexive and responsive to allow for interpretation. (It was intended therefore to use interviews to collect data.) Secondly, the sampling process advocated by Glaser and Strauss for the development of grounded theory is termed theoretical sampling, which they define as a:

> process of data collection for generating theory whereby the analyst jointly collects, codes and analyses his data and decides what data to collect next and where to find them, in order to develop his theory as it emerges.

The authors assert, therefore, that full coverage of the whole group is not required; depth is achieved not by numbers but by the collection and analysis of information from a selected group to achieve categories of data. In designing the study it was felt these methods and perspectives offered the flexibility to gather the information/data required to make an analysis.

In addition, the study design incorporated the process of triangulation, which Denzin (1970) describes as 'a plan of action that will raise the sociologist above the personalistic biases that stem from single methodologies'. The process of triangulation involves using either multiple methods, methodologies, data sources or investigators. The use of triangulation can increase the validity and reliability of the data collected and can form a sound basis for theory construction. The method chosen for the study described here was triangulation by data. This is achieved by collecting data from various sample groups (Webb, 1966). Themes and concepts are then derived from data which correlates from all sources.

IDENTIFYING RESPONDENTS

The study sought to triangulate data from three groups; PWAs, HCWs and key informants. It was important therefore that these groups be operationally defined at an early stage of the study. The latter two groups posed little problem in definition or access (see p. 51). Most pertinent to this discussion are the PWA Group. Whilst the medical definition of AIDS remains controversial and has undergone numerous changes, it is just as difficult for the researcher to define the group socially. Within the categories of 'homosexual' and 'drug addict' there is even greater diversity. Kinsey (1948) identified seven levels of homosexuality to which reference is still made today. There is also a difference between 'homosexual' and 'gay', the former was time consuming it was necessary in order to explain the study and to persuade those who were resisting my request. My previous career and training as a sales representative was extremely useful at this time. The rehearsed, smooth, personalized presentation, combined with a 'foot in the door' degree of persistence, was a winning formula.

It was not all one-sided as the process also involved what can only be described as a form of 'positive vetting' of me. Much of the initial interview time and discussion involved questions about me, my motivation, the purpose of my research and what would happen to the findings. Of major interest was my sexuality. Although I was never asked the question directly, most of those I approached for assistance sought to discover my sexual background. When it emerged during the discussion that I was not gay, the question would immediately turn to why I was conducting the study. There seemed to be an assumption that only gay people could, or should, conduct AIDS research. There are a number of implications for researchers in this assumption which cannot be developed here. However, it should have alerted me at the time to the problems I would face.

Another important area of concern related to who was funding the study and subsequently who had access and control of the data being collected. My sales training was used to the full in reassuring contacts. The outcome of the bargaining and negotiating was that there had to be some pay-off for respondents. In this case contacts were assured that the study was personally funded and data was accessible only to myself and my university supervisor. Also, a detailed report of the study and its findings would be sent to all participants and supporting organizations. An undertaking was also given that the study would only be published in whole or in part for academic purposes after a reasonable period of time.

OUTCOME OF THE PILOT STUDY

pilot revealed a number of problems related to sampling. the nature of the disease the population with AIDS very mobile. Most PWAs are single males living apart their families. What appears to occur when an individual posed HIV positive is that either he is rejected and

being considered the biomedical definition, whilst the latter is seen as acceptance and adoption of cultural attributes and lifestyle. Drug addicts also present a diverse group, dividing themselves by the type of drug, how and where used, and socially.

The main problem, however, is that most PWAs are hidden. Given the criminalization by society of drug abuse it could be argued that visible drug users outside of one's social circle or family are atypical. Carbello, Coxon and Micklin (1987) go further and suggest that any visible or accessible PWA is atypical.

Although theoretical sampling is not constrained by matching traditional variables and scientific rules, any study of PWAs must acknowledge the need for some form of cross-section sampling as a starting point. It must be remembered that AIDS is not a 'gay' disease. From a research perspective it is of no help to deny that risk groups do exist. I made a decision therefore to use the existing categories of risk groups from which to obtain a theoretical sample. The categories used were male homosexuals and bisexuals, IV drug abusers, heterosexual men and women and haemophiliacs. Although cross-categorization could arise this was not considered a problem in a theoretical sample. The aim was to achieve a cross-section for the study.

For the purposes of triangulation it was necessary to operationally define PWAs and other groups from whom data would be collected. These were:

- People with AIDS (PWAs) – any individuals who have been informed and acknowledge they have AIDS, a recognized HIV infection (PGL/ARC) or are HIV antibody positive.
- Health care workers (HCWs) – any individual within a health care delivery system engaged in a therapeutic and helping relationship with PWAs.
- Key informants (KIs) – individuals who, by virtue of their involvement with PWAs and AIDS issues, hold relevant information and insights not available from other sources.

Having decided who to sample the problem then arose of how to recruit respondents. Although the numbers of HCWs and KIs were small, they were not hidden. Most importantly, they were accessible. The PWA group posed special problems.

The author, having no connections with the gay or AIDS network, had to start from the position of 'outsider'.

Davies (1986) offers an overview of some of the sampling methods used to research gay men. These range from advertisements, published questionnaires in the gay press, selection by barmen to recruit respondents, snowballing, requests to gay organizations and covert strategies. Although some of these were feasible it was decided that, given the perspectives of the study and the resources available, the most fruitful approach would be to seek volunteers by making a direct approach to relevant organizations. However, due to the difficulties cited above, gaining access and cooperation would be crucial to the success of the study.

GAINING ACCESS

It was always recognized that the main problem in undertaking the study would be gaining access to the PWA target group. Although at the time of the study the potential number who fell within the PWA definition was approaching 2000, they were not easily accessible. As with any patient/client group they were diverse socially, medically and geographically.

There were two specific problems. First, the bulk of the PWA target group were located in the London area so finding PWAs to sample in the provinces would be extremely difficult. However, to be valid the study needed a wide geographical spread if it was not to be reduced to a study of the interaction of PWAs with health care in London. Second, unlike other defined patient groups, there was not one support group or national association who could provide a network to tap into.

Therefore a pilot study was undertaken to judge the feasibility of the project, the aims of which were to negotiate access, identify a sample frame and test the appropriateness of interviews as a research tool. The pilot also sought to identify gatekeepers. These are defined by Atkinson (1981) as 'actors with control over key resources and avenues of opportunity'. At this point the gatekeepers were thought to be local support and advocacy group organizers and medics.

To facilitate this stage of the study, requests were made throughout the Midlands region to AIDS support groups and support and advocacy groups representing other categories of

potential respondents. Despite numerous letters and telephone calls the requests drew a negative response. It emerged that such voluntary organizations usually have no paid organizer or executive head who was able to grant my request for access.

A second negative response came from the ethical committee secretary at a regional teaching hospital. I was informed that due to the political nature of AIDS, it was felt 'unwise' to receive such a request and that medical staff would resist attempts to conduct a 'non-scientific' study.

In an attempt to gain support similar requests were made at national level for assistance in gaining access to respondents. This also drew a negative response. I was passed from one department to another, given false leads, but most of all the people to whom I spoke were unable to make a decision. They were unaware of the degree of information that should be given and appeared to lack authority to allow access to respondents either directly or indirectly. The problem was compounded by trying to find out who was in charge or even who to contact. Some organizations were small, operated by volunteers from home, and some offered no correspondence address but only a telephone number which changed daily or weekly.

A further problem was who to ask. In 1988 *Gay Times* listed over 500 gay support organizations, 51 of which were for PWA and/or their friends and families. My preliminary attempts conduct a pilot did identify a small number of key organiza' who were sympathetic to the study. The only rem strategy was to approach the people at the top of these izations and work down. To my surprise access to individuals was relatively easy. They were helpful mative and, most importantly, supportive of th number of key national figures were all app responded in a similar way. This 'straight to the paid dividends; not only were the people w decisions identified but they appeared to be Contact with these individuals in effect be previously closed to me. Their support i and put me on equal terms with people sequently referred. I was no longer an

The process outlined above was f personal contact rather than corres

isolated by his family, friends and community or they rally round to support him. In either case the result is usually geographical relocation. A common reason given for geographical relocation from the provinces to London was to receive specialist medical treatment. Also, due to the overt discrimination directed towards PWAs and subsequently the need for confidentiality, most support organizations communicate by and record first names only and hold no addresses. The organization used were not, with one exception, structured membership organizations.

The result of these two factors was that PWAs may be in contact with support organizations for weeks or months but rarely years. Also, during this period the only means of contact and communication is if the individual attends support meetings or has volunteered his telephone number and address to the organizer. Therefore the population from which a sample may be drawn is unpredictable and continually changing as well as being hidden.

An added potential problem is the high morbidity and mortality rate of those affected by HIV and AIDS. Some of the voluntary organizers who were my contacts themselves had HIV or AIDS. This resulted in periods of hospitalization and lack of continuity. One important contact who was assisting in obtaining a sample died of AIDS, which meant that I had to restart the negotiation process with his replacement.

Another difficulty encountered during the pilot study was the lack of consistency amongst the contacts I was trying to make. In most of the organizations who were approached, staff were unpaid volunteers and subsequently changed functions as the demands required. Quite often people who had indicated they may be able to help were 'moved to other duties'.

STRATEGY FOR SAMPLING

Problems begin to arise

Despite the problems described above, contacts had been made and support in recruiting a volunteer sample was offered from key figures in the following organizations: Terence Higgins Trust (THT) Counselling Services; Front Liners, a support group within THT; the Haemophilia Society and two AIDS health workers employed by local authorities who ran a number of support groups. This process had taken almost three months but I felt secure that my contacts could fulfil their promises. All indicated that they had clients or members willing to be interviewed.

Negotiation with these organizations resulted in an open letter outlining the salient points and purpose of the study being drafted and circulated by these groups. The letter outlined the study in sufficient detail to allay anxieties about confidentiality, publication of results and what was expected of respondents. In essence the letter asked individuals to talk about their experiences with the health care system.

However, when the date for circulation and commencement of fieldwork arrived, some four months after initial contact, no volunteers responded. This resulted in another round of telephone calls and visits to put my foot in more doors in the hope that I could identify possible reasons. The problems appeared to be 'organizational' and not related to the study. As stated above, one key contact had died and his group appeared in a state of flux. Another group gave the intervening Christmas holiday as a reason, whilst another had two members die within two weeks which devastated remaining members. Meanwhile, the Haemophilia Society informed me that no members of its AIDS group had volunteered. A further problem arose from one of the AIDS health workers who began to waver in his support, questioning the ethics of recruiting from one of his support groups.

These problems caused long delays which were so serious that it was felt the study may have to be abandoned. At this point other methods of recruitment were considerred. However, time was of the essence and it was not considered feasible to start all over again.

During this time contact had been made with HCWs and KIs who were willing to participate. Although it was considered inappropriate to interview these groups first, some 'pilot' interviews did indicate deep distrust amongst PWAs towards both researchers and journalists. In pursuing this with contacts in the PWA groups, the depth of this distrust began to emerge. PWAs felt vulnerable to an ever growing group of outsiders and 'voyeurs' interested in this new fashionable topic. The only glimmer of hope at this stage was that some contacts indicated strong interest in the study amongst their members but an equally strong desire not to be visible.

The development and use of a questionnaire as a sampling strategy

Two methods of maintaining respondents' anonymity were considered. One method considered was telephone interviewing. However, this was not without its problems. Respondents would have to be willing to give out their telephone number, or contact, in this case to a faceless stranger. Another problem to contend with would be the ability to record and transcribe the interview. More straightforward, I felt, would be the distribution of an anonymous questionnaire.

The questionnaire used in the study had two purposes. Primarily it was developed as a means of access to a hidden sample group. It was felt that exposure to the research topic in this way would reduce the concerns and reticence being expressed. Secondly, the information gained from the questionnaire would produce baseline data related to interaction and relationships.

The questionnaire had four sections. The first dealt with biographical details and source of infection, followed by two sections looking at pre- and post-diagnosis interaction with the health care system. The final section allowed respondents to make comments and offer further information they considered relevant. Most importantly the final section contained an invitation for respondents to participate further by discussing with the researcher the experiences outlined in the questionnaire. An assurance was given that no other topics would be discussed. Respondents were asked to give their name and telephone number, or that of a third party, so they may be contacted. Alternatively, they could contact me via the address and telephone number given. Contacts readily agreed to distribute the questionnaires and a revised open letter to those within their network.

In total, 30 questionnaires and stamped addressed envelopes were distributed. Unfortunately distribution and response became protracted due to the nature of the groups, the frequency of their meetings, sickness and other unexplained delays. The first questionnaire was received in February and the last in

June. Subsequently interviews were conducted over the same period. Whilst this was very frustrating the intervening weeks did allow more than enough time for analysis and interviewing other HCWs and KIs.

During this period yet another problem arose; one contact withdrew his offer of help due to pressure of work which necessitated negotiations with a new source of help. During the fieldwork another reason for the delay emerged in that respondents waited and sought advice from their 'minders', usually their consultant, on whether to participate in the study.

The development and use of the questionnaire was highly successful. Twelve completed questionnaires were eventually returned, a further two were completed prior to interview by two individuals who volunteered after receiving the second open letter. A total of 14 questionnaires from the PWA group were used for analysis. These were returned from three major cities, Nottingham, London and Leeds. Nine respondents were interviewed, seven of whom volunteered using the questionnaire.

The profile of the group reflected the risk groups used. Only one of the nine respondents interviewed was female and only four were based in London. Five respondents attributed their infection to gay relationships, three to IV drug abuse, one of whom was unsure and felt it could have been attributed to heterosexual relationships. One respondent was a haemophiliac and attributed his infection to medical treatment.

The use of the questionnaire had by any measure been a success. In quantitative terms a 40% response rate had been achieved, 58% of whom agreed to be interviewed. In practical terms a sample had been obtained, access was gained and the study salvaged.

NEW PROBLEMS EMERGE

The difficulty now was how to materialize the promises of interviews made by respondents, given the geography to be covered and the nature of the sample. It was apparent at the design stage that respondents may not wish to be interviewed in their homes. Therefore elaborate arrangements were made to use neutral or other acceptable venues. The Terence Higgins

Trust had agreed that I could use their offices to interview respondents who did not wish to be interviewed at home. In addition one of the AIDS health workers made her office available to me and another his home. However, most beneficial were offices at a central London College of Nursing which had been made available to me at my request. Three respondents chose to be interviewed there.

These arrangements proved beneficial as only two respondents wished to be interviewed at home. However, it became problematic to reach an agreement for a time and place for interviews, even more so when being made through a third party. The frustration increased when respondents or contacts would make last minute changes. On some occasions respondents would fail to appear, either due to last minute problems or 'cold feet' or falling ill. When this happened the protracted process of arranging another interview began.

One particular respondent proved difficult and elusive. No less than four appointments were made and broken. The reasons varied, the last being that he felt he had been recognized in the reception of the College of Nursing – he promptly left the building. Although the respondents were in the main sick people and unable to predict their ability to participate at a given time, others were working and subject to limitations on their time.

However, another mechanism was involved. One respondent who had personally suffered at the hands of the media stated what in retrospect was obvious, that I was 'being tested out'. It was necessary for both respondents and contacts to be sure that my intentions were genuine. Another respondent felt I 'must be on the level to go to all this bother'.

There were, however, some benefits for the researcher in this complicated process. Repeated telephone calls certainly helped to 'break the ice' and develop rapport. Most importantly, it developed trust with vulnerable individuals and their advocates at a difficult time in the development of AIDS issues. Whilst my 'foot in the door' approach may have been seen by some as trying to coerce people into responding, it gave me an opportunity to sell myself and the benefits of the study. Over a period of time this contact and approach built up mutual respect and trust between me, my contacts and ultimately my respondents.

LESSONS TO BE LEARNT

This chapter has, I hope, identified some of the key issues in sampling hidden or inaccessible patient/client groups. Although the group discussed in this chapter were PWAs, there are analogies to be made with other patients or clients. The group could easily have been gay or lesbian nurses or doctors; health care workers in favour of euthanasia; patients who have taken a drug overdose, had abortions or any other patient group who may be stigmatized or marginalized by society or health care. Research on such groups can and must be undertaken if nurses and others are to understand the nature of the interaction of the patient with health care and the quality of the care given. Also, such research can be carried out successfully with minimal resources and lots of enthusiasm. It is also important to clearly define the target group(s) to be researched at an early stage of the study.

There are, however, some useful lessons for nurses and others to learn from this experience. Although the study design mirrored an accepted research process, the need for reflexivity is paramount. This became more apparent as the project progressed and confirms the point made by other researchers that it is not until you are in the field that research can be designed fully. These writers (Goffman, 1963; Becker, 1963) indicate that although the standard methodology textbooks suggest problem selection and research design are the first stages in the research process, design, collection of data and interpretation will change during fieldwork as they tend to take place simultaneously. To be rigid in the utilization of methods or methodologies would, I suggest, be detrimental to research with hidden or inaccessible groups, such as those mentioned above.

This chapter also reveals the successes and failures of pilot studies. The pilot revealed a number of actual and potential sampling problems, established a small network of contacts and aided the design of the study. However, it failed to identify the actual gatekeepers or to facilitate the degree of access required. On reflection, these were key failures. Whilst this could be attributed to the experience of the researcher I feel it is indicative of a more important issue.

Clearly extensive knowledge of or involvement with the target group would have been advantageous. This would have given a network of contacts to work from and 'inside information' of how the target group operated and who were the gatekeepers guarding access to them. Although Carbello, Coxon and Micklin (1987) insist that AIDS researchers need extensive knowledge of gay and AIDS lifestyles, the experience outlined in this chapter shows that whilst it is beneficial it is not essential. A study of this kind can be undertaken by an 'outsider'; indeed, there may even be advantages in doing so.

This chapter teaches, I hope, that naivety and lack of inside knowledge are not detrimental when combined with enthusiasm, openness and honesty. Had I tried to appear as someone other than a naive 'outsider' to my contacts and respondents, I am sure the outcome would not have been successful.

Finally the most valuable lesson to be learnt is to be creative in the application of research principles and processes irrespective of the model or methods being used. Whilst there are principles and guidelines underpinning all methods and methodologies, they should be seen and used as a tool, not a rule. Nurses especially should not be slaves to the medical/scientific model in the belief that this will lead to professional acceptability and credibility. It should be used where appropriate but there are other models and methods from a variety of disciplines which are, I would suggest, more appropriate and can inform us in more detail about what we do.

Nurses should choose from the wide range of methods available especially when researching difficult groups or topics. What is important in being creative and reflexive to the research area is that strategies are employed to ensure validity and reliability. It is essential that nursing research, as a young discipline, holds up well to scrutiny from within and outside the profession.

REFERENCES

Atkinson, P. (1981) Transition from school to working life, unpublished memorandum cited in *Ethnography: Principles and Practice*, (eds M. Hamersley and P. Atkinson), Tavistock, London.
Becker, H.S. (1963) *Outsiders*, Free Press, New York.
Carbello, M., Coxon, A.P.M., and Micklin, M. (1987) *Research on AIDS: Social Perspectives*, Working Paper No. 8, Project Stigma, University College, Cardiff.
Davies, P.M. (1986) *Some Problems in Defining and Sampling Non-*

Heterosexual Males, Working Paper No. 3, Project Stigma, University College, Cardiff.

Denzin, N.K. (1970) *Sociological Methods*, Butterworths, London.

Feldman, D.A. and Johnson, T.M. (1986) *The Social Dimensions of AIDS*, Praeger, New York.

Glaser, B. and Strauss, A. (1967) *The Discovery of Grounded Theory: Strategies for Qualitative Research*, Asline, Hawthorne, New York.

Goffman, E. (1963) *Stigma*, Prentice Hall, Englewood Cliffs, New Jersey.

Kinsey, A.C. (1948) *Sexual Behaviour in the Human Male*, Saunders, London.

Nolan, K.P. (1988) Patterns of interaction and relationships of people with AIDS and the health care system. Department of Sociology, University of Warwick. Dissertation.

Stacey, M. (1969) *Methods of Social Research*, Pergamon Press, Oxford.

Webb, E.J. (1966) Unconventionality, triangulation and inference, in *Sociological Methods*, (ed. N.K. Denzin), Butterworths, London.

5

Piloting a study

Alison Richardson

INTRODUCTION

The purpose of this chapter is to describe my experiences with a specific stage of the research process, the pilot study. It is a stage of the research process usually equated with exploration and often acknowledged as crucial to the success of any study. An illusion is readily created when reading research reports in a variety of journals that pilot work progresses with little mishap and that often only small amendments are acknowledged in relation to the design and instruments involved prior to instigation of the main project.

I will illustrate by recounting my own experience that the process of pilot work is often not straightforward and as a consequence hope to foster an appreciation of the complexities and dilemmas often encountered in such work. Evaluation of the process and results are crucial if any solutions are to be unravelled. Decisions concerned with the conceptual, ethical, methodological and analytical nature of the study may often cause the brain and heart to ache in tandem.

I consider few research procedures to be as useful as the pilot study, but prior to recounting my own experience I will devote a small amount of space to a consideration of the nature and purpose of pilot work.

GROUND WORK

No matter how diligent anybody strives to be when planning a research study, there will almost always arise a number of unanticipated problems. The effects of such problems, if not remedied at an early stage, may, if one is extremely lucky, turn out to be negligible but will probably reduce the amount of confidence which could be placed in the supposedly meaningful and reliable findings generated in the subsequent major study. At worst, the problems may unfortunately result in the complete abandonment of the study.

There thus appears strong reason for advocating the conduct of pilot work, if it enables the researcher to deal with any problems at an early stage and seek successful resolutions. It is perhaps then surprising that Prescott and Soeken (1989) consider pilot studies to be 'underdiscussed, underused and underreported'. This is disappointing, as information of such a nature would be extremely valuable to the practising researcher embarking on a project.

A number of terms have been utilized somewhat synonymously when referring to pilot work. Fox and Ventura (1983) describe it as a small scale study whereas Powers and Knapp (1990), in their dictionary of terms associated with research and theory, prefer the definition of 'a preliminary trial' of a research project. Alternatively Woods and Cantazaro (1988) use the term 'exploratory study' and Hogstel and Sayner (1986) envisage a pilot study to be a 'miniature version of a major research study'. These various terms thus imply that pilot work is often used to assess the feasibility of a planned study, the adequacy of instrumentation and problems in the proposed data collection strategy and method. Typically, mention is made of the fact that the participants will closely resemble those who will meet the criteria for inclusion in the main study.

Ort (1981) contends that a pilot study is conducted for one or more the following reasons:

- to determine the feasibility of the major study;
- to identify problems in the research design;
- to refine the data collection and analysis plan;
- to test the instrument to be used in the major study;
- to give the researcher some experience with the subjects, methodology and instruments.

In addition, and perhaps of greater consequence, there is the chance of revealing unexpected responses and findings which may suggest new directions for investigation or point out discrepancies in assumptions which need to be addressed and are fundamental to the project. However, such potential contributions should be tempered by a recognition of the limitations of pilot work. A limited sample is employed, it may not in fact reveal all the flaws associated with the design, instrument or methodology and there is the possibility to be considered that such work will deplete the available population of potential subjects.

The term pilot work is normally distinguished from that of pretesting, but they are often discussed together in research texts as separate but related concepts. Pretesting refers to the process of measuring the effectiveness of the instrument used to gather data. Obviously pretesting is often included in a pilot study or it may take place prior to such a study. A pilot study is thus often more comprehensive in purpose and outcome and incorporates the concept of pretesting data collection instruments along with the idea of a trial run of the study.

It is perhaps worth pointing out that on conducting a review of the literature and referring to the definitions preferred in the research texts already mentioned, it is evident that there generally exist two competing views about the nature and necessity for pilot work. The most commonly expressed philosophy about conducting a pilot study is that the whole research proposal should be energetically conducted on a small scale, thus resulting in a 'miniature version of the major research study, mimicking or resembling the major research in every detail' (Hogstel and Sayner, 1986) and facilitating a search for defects in the methodology and all components of the major study.

The nature of pilot work in this case constitutes a provision of a small scale test of a proposed complete study and is conducted after the research plan has been developed. Revisions are then made to the projected research based on the results of the pilot study. Yaremko *et al.* (1982) would like us to consider that it has other potential uses; in particular, pilot work can be designed to answer a methodological question and may be conducted prior to or as part of the development of a research plan. When used in this manner, pilot work (and perhaps it would be more cautiously viewed as preliminary work in this case) may serve as a guide to the development of a research plan instead of being a test of an already developed plan.

The necessity of diligently conducting a miniature small scale study on every occasion prior to performing a major study is open to debate and I tend to agree with the view of Lackey and Wingate (1989) who propose it is more plausible that if the researcher is experienced with the instruments and methodology used with a specific population, certain parts of a pilot study may be unnecessary. The necessity in this argument is thus dependent on the combination of data collection methods, technique, data analysis procedures and the researcher. If the researcher is lucky enough to be working with a familiar method and technique and the instrument is a standard one which has been used before with the population of the research, then there is no need for a pilot study. But many of us, I am sure, are placed in the unenviable position of working with an unfamiliar technique, a newly constructed instrument or an instrument which has been rearranged, with something added, deleted or more commonly patched together from a variety of instruments and having selected a particular population not subjected to prior research.

An aspect of particular relevance to my contribution to this text is the consideration of the 'publishability' of pilot work. Brink (1988) considers that pilot work outcomes should be viewed as insignificant and thus generally cannot be published, but draws a distinction concerned with the results of initial testing of research instruments. A publishable first study in Brink's opinion constitutes one which is concerned with uncovering new knowledge, one which constitutes a first step in a programme of research or a methodological test on a single instrument. Pilot studies should remain unpublished. Sidman (1960) offers a slightly more controversial opinion (in relation to experimental research) when advocating a study should not be published if it has been carried out and serious flaws have been exposed, and such a study should be considered a pilot study. However, a degree of clarification is offered by acknowledgement that publication of a pilot study is justified if a technique is discovered that would be valuable to other researchers or if new insights are developed about the research topics that have been alluded to in the previous literature.

I agree with a number of other authors (Burns and Grove, 1987; Seaman and Verhonick, 1982) that there are specific occasions when the total pilot study or selected parts of it should be widely disseminated, in particular those that relate to design, methodology and instrumentation. It is with this reassuring view that I overcome my apprehension in describing to you my experiences with pilot work, particularly when you learn that the opportunity for the project to flourish in the form of a major study did not materialize.

AN ENTHUSIASTIC START

Having furnished the reader with an appreciation of some of the theoretical constibutions and limitations attributable to pilot work which have been preferred by experienced nurse researchers, it is now timely to consider the efforts of a relatively novice researcher and my own experiences of conducting pilot work. The impetus for the proposed study stemmed from my clinical experience as a cancer nurse, with the additional motivation of conducting the research in part fulfilment for my studies for a Masters in Nursing (Richardson, 1989).

Nausea and vomiting associated with the administration of cytotoxic drugs is an intractable problem often encountered in the oncology setting. Whilst attempting to provide relief for this distressing and wretched experience it became obvious that the approaches available to the nurse appeared limited and often of minimal value. The pharmacological agents administered in attempts to abate the vomiting were disappointingly only partially effective and staff or patients with the skills or motivation to engage in behavioural techniques such as visualization and progressive muscle relaxation were scarce. In addition the physical and psychological environment for performing these activities were not readily available.

Thoughts were given to the potential contribution of the patient in this experience, particularly inspired by the previous research of Marilyn Dodd (1986). The involvement of patients in their care is a popular idea and it was considered possible that patient participation in assisting to control nausea and vomiting could lead to greater success in the management of this difficult problem.

A need was identified to explore whether patients perform self-care behaviours* in relationship to nausea and vomiting resulting from chemotherapy and whether these behaviours

* *Self-care behaviour:* Any activity personally initiated and performed by a patient for the purpose of helping to alleviate nausea and vomiting experienced due to chemotherapy.

were perceived as helpful. An outline of the relationship between the performance of self-care behaviours and the construct of exercise of self-care agency[†] would be profitable to pursue. Questions arose such as whether, when a patient experienced a greater degree of nausea and vomiting, they would perform an increased number of self-care behaviours or would become less effective in performing self-care as the symptoms worsen. These questions necessitated some answers. Literature suggested that the nausea and vomiting associated with chemotherapy may be viewed by the patient as a symptom complex not amenable to manipulation (possibly as a result of learned helplessness) or perhaps be perceived as a situation where personal involvement is not necessary (passive recipient), strengthened by the fact that intense symptoms will possibly only have to be endured for a short time.

The overall aim of the study was thus articulated, to explore some of the issues and outline a number of parameters associated with performance of self-care behaviours initiated to control chemotherapy induced nausea and vomiting, informed particularly by the conceptual framework of Dorothea Orem (1991), a prominent nurse theorist.

It was intended to achieve the proposed aim of the research by description and examination of several key areas.

- The nature, number and perceived effectiveness of self-care behaviours performed by patients to alleviate chemotherapy induced nausea and vomiting.
- The perceived occurrence, experience and distress associated with chemotherapy induced nausea and vomiting and the relationship, if any, to performance of self-care behaviours.
- The possibility of an association between performance of self-care behaviours and a high score on an instrument designed to measure exercise of self-care agency.
- Patients' sources of ideas for the chosen self-care behaviours.

A particular design and a number of instruments adapted from the work of previous American researchers (Dodd, 1987; Kierney and Fleischer, 1979; Rhodes et al., 1985) were selected and as a prelude to an anticipated larger main study, a pilot study was proposed.

[†] *Exercise of self-care agency*: The individual's self-appraisal of his or her power to engage in self-care actions, as measured by the Exercise of Self-Care Agency Scale developed by Kierney and Fleischer (1979).

The purpose of the pilot study was envisaged as providing some reassurance that the proposed design, method and sampling procedures would generate sufficient information to inform the areas outlined above. I made an assumption at this stage, an assumption which is, I envisage, a common one to the majority of novice researchers, that the pilot study would be conducted with little mishap, revealing only a few minor amendments to be made before conducting the major study.

What in fact materialized in this project were a number of phases of pilot work, allowing successive change and eventual refinement of the originally selected design and instruments. As a result of this sequential work following a certain degree of frustration and disillusion I eventually developed a healthy respect for the usefulness of such thorough pilot work.

I was encouraged by the thoughts of Jacobson (1988), who mentions that it may in fact be necessary to perform more than one pilot study and a multiphased series of pilot work may sometimes result. It did indeed, but by the time I reached my fourth in a search for an appropriate and meaningful design I think I can be forgiven for feeling a little despondent.

THE LONG DARK STRUGGLE

To return to the initial pilot study (now to be referred to as Phase 1), an interview had been selected as a means of detailing previous and current self-care behaviours utilized in a response to chemotherapy induced nausea and vomiting (at the first point of data collection) supplemented by a log to be completed approximately 24 hours following the administration of chemotherapy (the second point of data collection). Instruments to objectively estimate the degree of nausea and vomiting and exercise of self-care agency (ESCA) had also been selected, but for the purposes of this description I will confine myself to the development of the interview and the log (please refer to Figure 5.1 for a visual representation of the process of instrument development in its entirety).

Thoughts uppermost in my mind to be addressed during Phase 1 included whether the subjects would understand the questions and answer appropriately during the interview and what kind of difficulties would be encountered in arranging and conducting the research in the clinical setting. In addition I

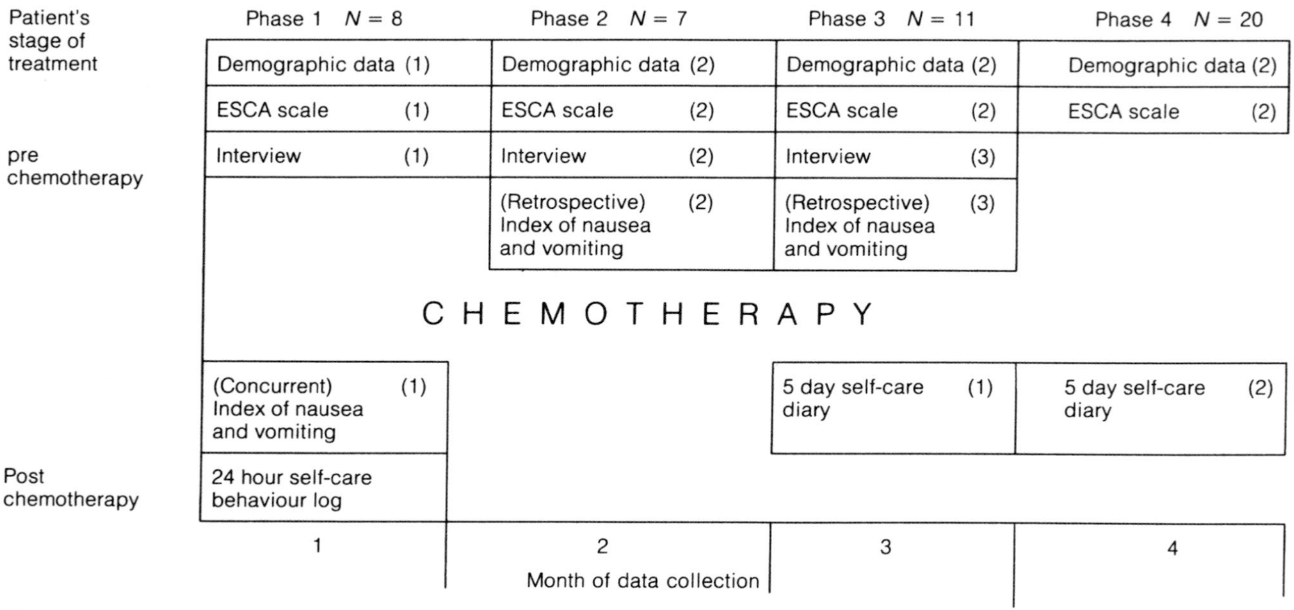

Patient's stage of treatment	Phase 1 N = 8	Phase 2 N = 7	Phase 3 N = 11	Phase 4 N = 20
pre chemotherapy	Demographic data (1)	Demographic data (2)	Demographic data (2)	Demographic data (2)
	ESCA scale (1)	ESCA scale (2)	ESCA scale (2)	ESCA scale (2)
	Interview (1)	Interview (2)	Interview (3)	
		(Retrospective) Index of nausea and vomiting (2)	(Retrospective) Index of nausea and vomiting (3)	
CHEMOTHERAPY				
Post chemotherapy	(Concurrent) Index of nausea and vomiting (1)		5 day self-care diary (1)	5 day self-care diary (2)
	24 hour self-care behaviour log			
Month of data collection	1	2	3	4

Figure 5.1 Process of instrument development – a flow diagram.
N.B. Numbers following each instrument denote version number.

Self-Care Behaviour Log

Directions:	Please complete the form overleaf. There are 3 parts.
Part 1	Refers to the actions you may have taken during this course of chemotherapy to help alleviate your nausea and vomiting, and requires that you jot these down. This may have included for example:

- alteration to your eating and drinking pattern
- resting and sleeping
- making yourself sick
- specific foods and drinks, please write down which
- distraction such as reading, listening to music and watching TV

Part 2	Please indicate the effectiveness of the action by circling the number which best describes its effectiveness in reducing your nausea and vomiting.
Part 3	Please write down the source of idea for your action, for example yourself, a friend, a nurse or family member.

Part 1	*Part 2*				*Part 3*
Actions taken	Effectiveness of actions				Source of idea for actions
	Not relieved at all	Partly relieved	Nearly completely relieved	Completely relieved	
A _____	0	1	2	3	a _____
B _____	0	1	2	3	b _____
C _____	0	1	2	3	c _____
D _____	0	1	2	3	d _____

Figure 5.2 An illustration of the log utilized in Phase 1.

was keen to gain experience in working with the selected instruments and with the subjects chosen for inclusion in the study, possibly developing a smooth and confident technique for administration of the interview and standardizing the approach to recruitment and data collection.

The results of Phase 1 raised several serious concerns. The interview was muddled and conducted with little flexibility. It appeared to confuse subjects as a result of switching the line of questioning quickly from nausea to vomiting in terms of the extent of the problem and then returning to nausea in terms of self-care behaviours utilized – progressing to those self-care behaviours performed in response to vomiting. As a result of this approach subjects were unable to formulate ideas and concentrate on one line of enquiry at a time. Subjects appeared to hold a very poor recall of the performance of any self-care behaviours in relationship to post-chemotherapy nausea and vomiting and thus minimal data were generated.

The log utilized at the second point of data collection (Figure 5.2) for the purpose of recording self-care behaviours performed on this occasion of receiving chemotherapy appeared in principle easy and effective to complete. However, I became concerned about approaching subjects and collecting data at a time when they were obviously at great risk of experiencing nausea and vomiting, potentially incapacitated by these and other adverse effects of chemotherapy. It seemed tactless and unacceptable on my behalf to question respondents closely on this sensitive topic whilst particularly acknowledging a psychosocial component to chemotherapy induced nausea and vomiting. The recall of self-care behaviours in this particular time period (24–36 hours post-chemotherapy) was also possibly hampered by the sedative/amnesic effects of the anti-emetic drugs administered, a point not considered prior to Phase 1 nor mentioned by previous researchers in this field. Subjects thus failed to respond to the instruments in the manner envisaged.

However, positive contributions to the study had also been realized during Phase 1. It reaffirmed the realistic sampling criteria selected on consultation with the physicians concerned and provided encouragement of the likelihood of reaching the anticipated sample size in the time available (expected N = 50). Both the medical and nursing personnel in the clinical areas concerned responded to the purpose of the study favourably and with encouragement which helped enormously when trying to identify potential recruits and organizing a mutually agreeable time for approaching the proposed subject.

It also became clear that a substantial amount of time and energy was required to arrange and conduct the data collection. Subjects often proved elusive due to long absences from the clinical area whilst attending various tests and investigations which are necessary when receiving chemotherapy. When subjects had been located they were often involved in being interviewed by medical and nursing personnel. After some detective work it appeared that at the first point of data collection, the time periods of 11.00 am to midday and 1.00 pm to 4.00 pm appeared to be the most profitable for gaining the subjects' attention. This element was magnified due to the incorporation of two points for data collection and at the second point, the approach had to be expertly timed, balanced between not disturbing the subject if they were resting during or following the administration of chemotherapy and catching them before they left the hospital. Often subjects were desperate to leave as soon as possible and this often occurred early in the morning, following the termination of the chemotherapy.

On a more personal level, during Phase 1 I began to gain important insights concerned with the nature of approaching patients as subjects for research and the development of skills associated with competent interviewing. I was nervous and to some extent doubtful about my abilities in this respect. Phase 1 led to a ready indication of the research related strengths and limitations of the clinical setting in which the study was taking place. However, I felt I had been naive in holding the expectation that the provisional selection of instruments would provide immediate answers and generate the anticipated quantity and quality of data and this necessitated the development of Phase 2.

I entered Phase 2 feeling extremely anxious and conscious that any search for a more successful method of data collection would be limited by the time available for the project and perhaps more importantly by my own personal resources. The interview was significantly modified, a number of questions were deleted which had been perceived as not being understood by the subjects or having been poorly stated and producing irrelevant data/discussion and partial answers. Obtaining complete and understandable responses had not proved as easy as anticipated. The schedule in Phase 1 was felt to contain a badly organized and illogical sequence of questioning. A more logical progression of questioning was developed and a more open approach was utilized, with a greater use of probes, to explore and encourage subjects to talk about behaviours which were sometimes perceived as insignificant actions. I was conscious, however, that this degree of probing may not always be consistent and could significantly bias replies. A smoother technique was developed for framing the interview and I became more confident in developing a rapport and clarifying instructions to the respondents. Tactics to elicit separate information about the behaviours performed for the symptoms of nausea (feeling sick) and vomiting (being sick) were developed, in addition to pursuing information concerned with both preventive and reactive self-care behaviours.

The second point for data collection, post-chemotherapy, was for the present abandoned, for the reasons discussed previously. Data collection now occurred at one point in time prior to chemotherapy. The interview was relied upon to elicit all the information concerned with the performance of self-care behaviours, with recognition that this approach would hamper reliability due to the potentially significant effects of defective memory recall.

Self-Care Diary

It may be difficult for you to recall the things you do to help you cope with your nausea and vomiting. Please can you note down any things you do over the next five days and then send the completed diary back to me in the envelope provided. *Day 1* is the day you receive your chemotherapy.

Directions: Please complete the form overleaf. There are 3 parts.

Part 1 Refers to the actions you may take each day to help alleviate your nausea and vomiting, and requires that you jot these down. Please mark down any actions, however simple you may feel they are.

Part 2 Please indicate the effectiveness of the action by circling the number which best describes its effectiveness in reducing your nausea and vomiting.

Part 3 Please write the source of idea for your action, for example yourself, a friend, a nurse or family member.

Part 1 Actions taken	Part 2 Effectiveness of actions				Part 3 Source of idea for actions
	Not relieved at all	Partly relieved	Nearly completely relieved	Completely relieved	
A _____	0	1	2	3	a _____
B _____	0	1	2	3	b _____
C _____	0	1	2	3	c _____
D _____	0	1	2	3	d _____

Figure 5.3 An illustration of the log utilized in Phase 3.

On evaluating Phase 2, I became more and more convinced that the respondents found it difficult to recall self-care behaviours performed in response to nausea and vomiting but evidence from Phase 1 generated from the log indicated there was a variable degree of activity post-chemotherapy. The emphasis of study began to shift considerably at this juncture. I returned to the idea of a log, but this would be extended to collect information about the performance of behaviours over a longer period of time (five days) commencing the day the respondents received chemotherapy and following the subjects on discharge home (Figure 5.3). This time period was chosen after some thought and recourse to the literature, indicating that nausea and vomiting subside over this time period and in some patients disappear. The diary was of a simple, highly structured format and developed to judge the effectiveness of this method of data collection in eliciting information concerned with self-care and the adequacy of the accompanying instructions, along with the likely response rate.

I was sightly sceptical as to the motivation required by the subjects to complete such an instrument on a daily basis with no contact from the researcher following discharge home. This phase, however, would serve as an accurate estimate of the amount of missing data and sample attrition which may be encountered with such a method. The literature on the utilization of diaries as research instruments provided evidence that a structured approach tended to produce a higher return rate and mentioned several strategic and structural considerations for ensuring completion and retrieval. However, this information had to be considered in light of the fact that the majority of previous studies utilized a relatively healthy population who were attending general practitioner surgeries and reporting minor health problems and self-care strategies (Freer, 1980; Roghmann and Haggerty, 1972).

The diary was constructed in three parts dealing with self-care behaviour performed, effectiveness of such action and source of idea for each action respectively and this information was recorded daily. A stamped addressed envelope was provided to return the diary to me at the close of the data collection period. Eleven diaries were given to subjects and nine were returned. I was immediately heartened by the response rate and surprised at the detail contained in the responses. In addition, a number of handwritten replies accompanied the diaries, recounting how useful they found the diary keeping and providing additional information.

LIGHT AT THE END OF THE TUNNEL

In Phase 4 I elected to develop and refine the diary approach and compare the quantity and quality of data obtained using a single instrument, the diary, as opposed to the combination of interview and diary. The diary had produced promising data in Phase 3 and I was inclined to favour the diary as the sole instrument for data collection. The interview in Phase 3 had again failed to produce worthwhile data and was therefore deleted.

It had not been envisaged when commencing this study that it would prove so necessary to try out more than one method of data collection to help decide on an appropriate method. Following previous disappointments and left with the realization that the major study would not be possible in the time remaining, I attempted to enter Phase 4 with a renewed enthusiasm, hoping to ensure that it would culminate in an instrument worth the investment of time and energy so far devoted to the project.

Nausea as a sole symptom rather than the symptom complex of nausea and vomiting was selected for description in Phase 4 (Figure 5.4). Vomiting often subsides shortly following chemotherapy, but nausea can remain an intractable problem on discharge home. In addition to recording the actions taken, effectiveness of actions and indication of source of idea, an evaluation of the intensity of nausea and associated distress was recorded by the respondent. This was included so attempts could be made to describe the correlations between severity of nausea and the propensity to perform self-care. Phase 3 had previously revealed a weakness in the instructional aspects of the diary; instructions stated that the respondent should commence completion of the diary the day following chemotherapy administration. It had been assumed by the researcher that this would also constitute the day of discharge home. What in fact transpired is that a number of subjects remained in hospital for a variable period, perhaps for a blood transfusion

Self-Care Diary

Directions: Day 1 is the day you leave hospital. Please complete the diary each evening, for five days, and then place the complete diary in the envelope and send it back to me.
The diary is in five parts.

Part 1 Please circle the statement which most clearly corresponds to your experience today.

Part 2 Please circle the statement which most clearly corresponds to your experience today.

Part 3 Requires you to record any actions you may have taken today to help alleviate your nausea. For example:

- Taking antisicknes pills
- Alteration to your eating and drinking pattern, such as avoiding food
- Eating specific foods
- Drinking specific drinks

Part 4 Please indicate the effectiveness of your actions in relieving your nausea by circling the appropriate statement.

Part 5 Please record the source of idea for your action. For example, yourself, a friend, a nurse or family member.

Day 1 (The day you leave hospital)

Part 1 – Severity of nausea

| I did not feel nauseated | I felt nauseated for one hour or less | I felt nauseated for two or three hours | I felt nauseated for four or six hours | I felt nauseated continuously |

Part 2 – Distress from nausea

| I did not feel any distress from nausea | I felt mild distress from nausea | I felt moderate distress from nausea | I felt great distress from nausea | I felt as severe distress from nausea as can be |

Part 3 – Actions taken to relieve nausea

Part 4 – Effectiveness of actions

| Nausea not relieved at all | Nausea partly relieved | Nausea nearly completely relieved | Nausea completely relieved |

Part 5 – Source of idea for actions

Figure 5.4 An illustration of the log utilized in Phase 4.

or awaiting transport home. Thus in Phase 4, the instructions were amended to read 'on the day of your discharge home'.

This final phase proved the most successful and few problems were encountered. Of the 20 diaries distributed, 16 were received back by the researcher. I considered this a highly satisfactory return rate, but of course was unable to probe for any failures to respond. In retrospect this would have been a useful procedure but would have entailed telephoning the respondents at home or ensuring they were followed up when returning for a further course of chemotherapy. I considered this unreasonable and subjects may have felt hounded.

At the completion of each phase data were analysed descriptively but owing to the small number of subjects accrued in each phase it was not possible to seek correlations within the data. However, opportunity did arise to obtain some indication as to potential sample size that would be necessary in any major study to maximize chances of obtaining data which displayed a certain degree of variability in terms of fluctuations in levels of nausea, the number of self-care behaviours performed and scores attributable to exercise of self-care agency.

The analysis also revealed that it would perhaps be prudent in any major study to develop a means of attributing a ratio of effectiveness to self-care behaviours. The pilot work was successful in providing a great deal of information on the nature of the study variables and revealed possibilities for future attempts at a more sophisticated analysis relevant to the level of measurement achievable. Routes for analysing the data more efficiently and the development of appropriate methods of coding and recording transpired, uplanned steps I had not foreseen at the start. It is proposed that any future study would possibly utilize the diary form illustrated in Figure 5.5. Through the four phases of pilot work I feel I was able eventually to produce a convincing argument for utilizing a diary approach as an acceptable and worthwhile method of describing self-care behaviour associated with post-chemotherapy nausea (and potentially holding a degree of validity and reliability).

SALVAGE WORK

In conclusion, I consider the phases of pilot work provided a creative attempt to devise the most appropriate research method and select relevant data collection tools in relationship to illustrating the behaviours which cancer patients utilize to assist them in dealing with the nausea and vomiting which result as a consequence of chemotherapy. In addition and

Self-Care Diary

Day 1 (The day you leave hospital)

Part 1 – Severity of nausea

I did not feel nauseated	I felt nauseated for one hour or less	I felt nauseated for two or three hours	I felt nauseated for four or six hours	I felt nauseated continuously

Part 2 – Distress from nausea

I did not feel any distress from nausea	I felt mild distress from nausea	I felt moderate distress from nausea	I felt great distress from nausea	I felt as severe distress from nausea as can be

Part 3 – Actions taken to relieve nausea

Actions taken to relieve nausea	Effectiveness of actions				Source of idea for actions
	0 Not relieved at all	1 Partly relieved	2 Nearly completely relieved	3 Completely relieved	
A _____	0	1	2	3	a _____
B _____	0	1	2	3	b _____
C _____	0	1	2	3	c _____
D _____	0	1	2	3	d _____

Figure 5.5 Proposed format of diary for any future research project.

perhaps of greater significance, it prompted me to focus some thought on a number of interesting aspects which had surfaced, concerned with the nature and consequences of symptoms attributable to disease and therapy. It was more complex than I had first envisaged with a multitude of variables involved which would prove difficult to tease out in any later study. As examples, I questioned what the consequences may be of the person being in a home or hospital environment in relationship to the motivation to perform self-care behaviours, whether there are discriminating factors involved when people take decisions to perform self-care when symptoms are attributable to therapy rather than disease. Thus it is possible, as described by Hinds and Gattuso (1991), that the outcome of pilot work often may refocus subsequent research, subtly or in a more major manner.

The sequential phases of pilot work described in the previous

pages I hope can be considered as holding a number of powerful contributions to any future work in this field, particularly
when the work is considered in combination with the available
literature. Searching the literature concurrently as the pilot
work progressed led to a number of different foci developing
during the phases of pilot work, which ultimately informed the
development of the next phase. The phases of any study are
almost always interactive, not performed in sterile isolation,
and often development proceeds simultaneously with decisions
regarding one phase affecting decisions made at another. This
was certainly a feature of my work. The major components of
the study impinged on the design, measures and data analysis.

As a result of my experiences I am convinced that more
attention devoted to pilot work will undoubtedly increase the
time spent in preparation for any major study; however, I
believe this will be time well invested as the experience will
assist the researcher and provide opportunity to modify any
proposals whilst it is still feasible to do this, which is not
possible after the study has been executed.

On a personal note the disappointment and frustration that
transpired as a result of not proceeding to conduct a major study
has been subdued by utilization of many of the methodological
insights that evolved as a consequence of the phase of pilot
work described. I hope the publication of these pilot outcomes
in a somewhat abbreviated form will contribute a small piece
to the jigsaw which constitutes the reality of the research
experience.

REFERENCES

Brink, P. (1988) The pilot study (editorial). *Western Journal of Nursing
    Research*, **10**(3), 237–8.
Burns, N. and Grove, S. (1987) *The Practice of Nursing Research: Conduct,
    Critique and Utilisation*, W.B. Saunders, Philadelphia.
Dodd, J. (1987) *Managing Side Effects of Chemotherapy and Radiotherapy*,
    Appleton & Lange, Norwalk, Connecticut.
Dodd, M. (1986) Self care in patients with cancer, in *Issues and Topics in
    Cancer Nursing*, (eds R. McCorkle and G. Hongladarom), Appleton-
    Century-Crofts, Norwalk, Connecticut.
Fox, R. and Ventura, M. (1983) Small scale administration of instru-
    ments and procedures. *Nursing Research*, **32**(2), 122–5.
Freer, C. (1980) Self care: a health diary study. *Medical Care*, **18**(8),
    853–61.

Hinds, P. and Gattuso, J. (1991) From pilot work to a major study in cancer nursing research. *Cancer Nursing*, **14**(3), 132–5.

Hogstel, M. and Sayner, N. (1986) *Nursing Research*, McGraw Hill, New York.

Jacobson, S. (1988) Evaluating instruments for use in clinical nursing research, in *Instruments for Clinical Nursing Research*, (ed. M. Frank-Stromborg), Appleton and Lange, Norwalk, Connecticut.

Kierney, B. and Fleischer, B. (1979) Development of an instrument to measure exercise of self care agency. *Research in Nursing and Health*, **2**(1), 25–34.

Lackey, N. and Wingate, A. (1989) The pilot study: one key to research success, in *Advanced Design in Nursing Research*, (eds P. Brink and M. Wood), Sage Publications, Newbury Park.

Orem, D. (1991) *Nursing: Concepts of Practice*, 4th edn C.V. Mosby, St. Louis.

Ort, S. (1981) Research designs: pilot study, in *Readings for Nursing Research*, (eds S. Krampitz and N. Pavlovich), C.V. Mosby, St. Louis.

Powers, B. and Knapp, T. (1990) *A Dictionary of Nursing Theory and Research*, Sage Publications, Beverly Hills, California.

Prescott, P. and Soeken, K. (1989) The potential uses of pilot work. *Nursing Research*, **38**(1), 60–62.

Rhodes, V., Watson, P. and Johnson, M. (1985) Patterns of nausea and vomiting in chemotherapy patients: a preliminary study. *Oncology Nursing Forum*, **12**(3), 42–8.

Richardson, A. (1989) SelfCare. A study of the behaviours initiated by chemotherapy patients to control nausea and vomiting. King's College, University of London. Unpublished MSc thesis.

Roghmann, K. and Haggerty, R. (1972) The diary as a research instrument in the study of health and illness behaviour. *Medical Care*, **10**(2), 143–63.

Seaman, C. and Verhonick, P. (1982) *Research Methods*. Appleton-Century Crofts, Norwalk, Connecticut.

Sidman, M. (1960) Pilot studies, in *Tactics of Scientific Research*, (ed. M. Sidman), Basic Books, New York.

Woods, N. and Cantazaro, M. (1988) *Nursing Research: Theory and Practice*, C.V. Mosby, St. Louis.

Yaremko, R., Harari, H., Harrison, R. and Lynn, E. (1982) *Reference Handbook of Research Statistical Methods in Psychology: For Students and Professionals*, Harper and Row, New York.

6

Trial and error: an experiment in practice

Richard McMahon

INTRODUCTION

'The meteoric rise and regrettably slower fall of many a form of treatment bear eloquent witness to the lack of the controlled trial in medicine.' It was thus that the Editor of the *British Medical Journal* indicated in 1948 the great importance he placed on the first randomized controlled trial to be published in that journal (Editorial, 1948; Medical Research Council, 1948). The randomized controlled trial replaced previous forms of evaluation of new treatments which had been largely based on the observed outcomes for patients given a new intervention, compared with the clinician's memory of patients treated under the old treatment. Unless the outcome for the new treatment was startlingly better, the accuracy of the evaluation was haphazard to say the least.

The use of the experimental method in nursing research is viewed by some, both inside and outside the occupation, as a sign of the maturing of the academic side of the discipline. Others view it as an unwanted move towards reductionism and as such should have no place in the study of what they consider to be a predominantly interaction based activity. Although some see the randomized controlled trial as the epitome of good science, much of nursing does not lend itself to this form of investigation, which has led to a schism among some researchers between those supporting these qualitative and quantitative approaches (Corner, 1991). However, there are activities in nursing and midwifery which are best investigated using this method, with some spectacular successes (e.g. Sleep and Grant, 1988).

I chose to use an experiment in my study to investigate a commonly occurring skin problem for a number of reasons. First, having completed a previous study which was supervised from a department of sociology which had an enviable reputation for the excellence of its qualitative research, I felt that I wanted to gain some expertise in quantitative methodology. Secondly, I was looking for a study for which the basic research question was generated from practice and having identified my subject, soon realized that the only way to address some of the questions satisfactorily was through an experiment. Thirdly I thought such a study would be fairly straightforward in that there are basic principles which must be adhered to if a study is to be a true experiment and that with the 'number-crunching' facilities provided by modern computer technology, the analysis of the data would be relatively easy and less time consuming than the laborious approach often required in qualitative research.

This chapter is therefore about my experiences of planning and performing what turned out to be a somewhat unconventional randomized controlled trial. I believe that many of the problems I experienced are not unique to this study; rather they may be faced by many nurses embarking on an experiment.

Theory of experiments

Polit and Hungler (1987) identify three characteristics of 'true' experiments, namely manipulation, control and randomization. Manipulation refers to the deliberate altering of the independent variable by the investigator, after which the resultant change in the dependent variable is then measured. Control refers to the method of ensuring that the change in the dependent variable can only be attributed to the manipulation of the independent variable. This traditionally takes the form of a second group of patients or items being investigated, identical to the first, except that the independent variable does not get manipulated. The best way to ensure that the two groups are similar in as many aspects as possible and to make sure that any intentional or unintentional bias by the experimenter cannot affect which group and individual patient is put into is by randomly allocating the subjects to the groups.

Another aspect of clinical trials which is designed to neutralize bias by those involved in the study is that of 'blinding'. This refers to the withholding of information from certain people as to which group particular patients have been allocated to. Dumas (1987) identifies the three groups of individuals who are kept in the dark in single, double and treble blind trials; namely the patient, those administering the intervention and anyone else involved in evaluating outcomes, such as laboratory staff. However, as Dumas points out, it is extremely difficult to achieve more than single blind experiments in any studies other than drug trials. The reason for this is that most nursing interventions are difficult to disguise. The pressure to introduce blinding to trials has on occasions lead to ridiculous situations; for example, in the study by Ormiston *et al.* (1985) the purple treatment of gentian violet was compared with the yellow treatment of Iodosorb in a trial to evaluate which was more effective in the treatment of leg ulcers. The researchers claimed that those evaluating the healing were unaware of which treatment group individual patients were in, in an effort to present a respectable double blind trial. This was despite the obvious implausibility of the claim unless the nature of blindness in the trial was an inability of the evaluators to differentiate between yellow and purple.

Purpose and advantages of trials

The purpose of an experiment is to show whether or not a causal relationship exists between two variables; that is, a hypothesis is tested. No other methodology can logically lead to an answer which 'proves' such a relationship. For example, where two groups are investigated and compared but there is no manipulation of a variable, it is never possible to be completely confident of cause and effect. This has been demonstrated in the nuclear power debate, where initial research showed that a correlation existed between the incidence of certain types of cancer and the presence of a nuclear power station near the community (Forman *et al.*, 1987). However, this did not *prove* a link between the two and subsequent research has shown a similar correlation between the incidence of cancers in communities and sites where nuclear power stations were planned but never built (Cook-Mozaffari *et al.*, 1989). This demonstrates the inherent weakness of correlational research but frequently it is the only method open to the researcher; for example, the smoking–lung cancer link has for obvious reasons never been 'proved' by experiment, only suggested by correlational studies.

Therefore, the strength of experiments lies in their ability to show cause and effect beyond reasonable doubt. But for nurses at this time there are other advantages in choosing such a methodology. In my case I am convinced that one of the reasons why I was successful when I applied to the regional health authority for funding was that the panel of consultants who were interviewing me could understand and identify with the project. A friend and colleague who has similar credentials and communication skills to me was unsuccessful with a project which I believe has far more wide-reaching implications than mine; mainly, I suspect, because his study was ethnographic – a methodology which by definition is alien to scientists. Regardless of the rights or wrongs of such an outcome, there is money for clinical trials and when I approached pharmaceutical companies for support, again they were sympathetic.

ABOUT THE STUDY

Overview

The problem that I had encountered in practice which prompted the research project was that of inflamed skin beneath the breasts of female patients I was nursing in hospital. I felt that this would make a good topic to investigate as it appeared to be an easily defined subject which was important to the patients who suffered with it and a simple literature search indicated that there was little previous relevant research. As it turned out appearances were deceptive as it was a complex problem, involving multiple variables and conflicting advice in respected textbooks.

As there was no previous nursing literature relating to the problem and only limited work from other disciplines, it was clear that before any work could be done on evaluating different treatments, it was necessary to find out the prevalence of the problem, to determine what constitutes current nursing practice and to establish how much of a problem this condition is to the patients who have it. Initially it had felt tiresome to have to do so much preliminary work as I had a strong desire to start the experiment. However, the exploratory work not only produced several surprising findings but also the evidence which justified performing the experiment. This evidence was invaluable when the trial ran into difficulties.

Exploratory work

Point prevalence study

The first part of the study was designed to clarify whether the problem of inflamed sub-mammary skin was as widespread as my hunch told me it was. There was no useful literature to support my feelings and it would clearly be useless to embark on an experiment if the chances of finding sufficient participants was low. Therefore I decided to approach this by performing a point prevalence study. This involved sending 15 data collectors to each of the 131 wards in every speciality and unit in the District on one day. This work (McMahon, 1991) showed a much higher prevalence than I had expected, with 5.8% of all adult female inpatients being found to have a sub-mammary skin lesion on that day and a further 5.4% had had a lesion during their current admission which had healed subsequently. Having found 65 patients with lesions in the District in one day, I was confident that I would have no difficulty recruiting 75–100 patients in one year to support the experiment.

Ward sister's questionnaire

The second part of the exploratory phase had the purpose of trying to identify and quantify current nursing practice to treat this problem. To achieve this, the ward sisters and primary nurses throughout the District were sent a questionnaire asking them what they knew about sub-mammary skin problems, how they treated them and with what success. This study showed that, as in the treatment of pressure sores in the past (Murray, 1988), over 100 different treatments were in use, indicating that no one treatment had emerged as a result of trial and error practice.

Patient interviews

The third part of the exploratory phase was to interview patients. This aspect of the study had a number of purposes. Firstly, it provided some survey data on patients' experiences of having a sub-mammary lesion. Secondly, by asking open questions which prompted a variety of answers, it was possible to establish the range of answers that might be given by other respondents to these questions and to use this information to develop response sets for the researcher to tick when interviewing patients on entering them into the trial. A number of surprising findings did emerge from this part of the study; for example a suprising proportion of patients (28%) had first started getting sore skin beneath their breasts when they were less than 30 years old.

Experimental phase

The experimental phase of the research involved randomizing patients with submammary lesions who were in hospital to receive different nursing interventions. Five nursing interventions were chosen for use in the trial, including plain soap and water which was the control or comparison treatment. The remaining four interventions were the three most popular treatments reported in the ward sister's questionnaire (talc, inserting gauze and applying Drapolene) and a hydrocolloid patch for which there was reasonable theoretical and practical evidence that it might be effective. As most of the lesions are bilateral, it is possible to test two interventions on the same patient, one under each breast. This has many advantages, as variables such as age, weight and so on are controlled.

The randomization took place after specimens had been taken from the affected area for microbiological testing and the lesions had been measured, described and photographed. The patients were then followed up after two, seven, 14 and 28 days. The processing of the microbiological specimens took place in the local Public Health Laboratory. The challenges that the experimental phase presented form the basis for the rest of this chapter.

TESTING MORE THAN TWO VARIABLES

The questionnaire to ward sisters and primary nurses had shown that a large number of different interventions were in current use by nurses. Although some of them were only mentioned once or twice, a reasonable number such as inserting gauze between the surfaces and using talc were mentioned relatively frequently. Randomized controlled trials are often thought of as testing one treatment either against a control ('no' treatment) group or against a comparison ('traditional' treatment) group. However, advice from two different statisticians offered two ways of conducting a trial which compared several variables. The first method suggested was to use the 'sequential sampling design'. This involved starting with two interventions and performing a number of 'little' experiments. This meant randomizing one participant at a time to each

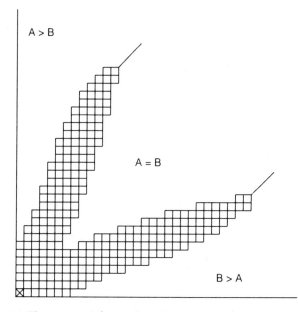

Figure 6.1 The sequential sampling design grid.

treatment to the left and right breasts and recording the outcome on a chart, such as that shown in Figure 6.1.

If both breasts healed equally well, the trial was considered to be tied and the result was not entered on the grid. If treatment A was more effective, then an X was to be placed above the cross in the bottom left hand corner. If B was more successful, then the X was to be put in the box to the right of that square. The results of the little experiments would continue to be recorded in this way until an X enters one of the three white areas. Entering the white area in the middle would indicate no statistically significant difference between the two interventions. The white area above the grid would indicate that treatment A is significantly more effective than B and vice versa for the area below the grid. Maybe the one criterion which could have been used was time to total healing; however, this would have meant visiting every patient every day, something which the part time researchers could not do.

It is apparent that in the grid shown in Figure 6.1, it is possible to get a conclusion after as few as seven 'little' experiments and certainly after 22. The advantages of this design are attractive. Firstly, from an ethical point of view it is always problematic that at the end of an experiment when one treatment is found to have been successful, the experimenter has inflicted a less beneficial treatment on around half the participants. (An example is provided by the Bristol Cancer Centre trial (Carlisle, 1991; Bagenal *et al.*, 1990).) With the sequential sampling design, once a result has been reached the study can stop, preventing any further patients being randomized to the 'unsuccessful' treatment. The successful treatment can then be compared with a different intervention until one of those proves better and so on. Secondly, the issue at first sight of having some form of a result after, at most, the 22nd participant is attractive as it ensures that some form of conclusive result is obtained from a relatively small sample; a larger sample allowing more interventions to be tested.

Unfortunately I felt that the design was unsuitable for this study for two reasons. Firstly, as the effectiveness of the nursing treatments in this experiment was to be judged on a number of variables, such as the size of the lesions, the quantity of bacteria on the skin surface and the subjective degree of discomfort they caused, it could be extremely difficult to decide that one

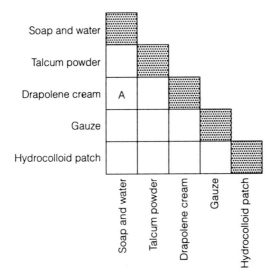

Figure 6.2 The incomplete block design.

treatment was 'better' than the other. For example, one treatment might result in making the lesion less uncomfortable, but not necessarily alter the number of bacteria. Similarly the affected area might reduce slightly more quickly under one treatment, but what degree of change in a ratio variable would constitute a 'win' for that intervention? Without a clear criterion of which intervention has 'won' in the little experiment, it is not possible to use the grid. The second reason was that results can only be entered on the grid if there *is* a definite 'winner'. Therefore, the idea that the maximum number of patients required would be 22 is false as, if there is little difference in outcome between the two (as could be highly likely in this trial), then that result would not get entered on the grid.

Therefore, the second design was chosen. This consisted of setting up an 'incomplete block' design. Under this design the interventions were paired by using a grid, as in Figure 6.2. Each of the unshaded cells represents a pair of interventions which are applied to a patient. For example, the patient associated with cell A would be treated with Drapolene cream on one area and soap and water on the other. There are disadvantages to this approach too. For example, every one of the cells must be completed before another grid can be started and only completed grids can be analysed. The analysis of those grids involves sophisticated statistical methods such as general linear modelling and either a good understanding of computer statistics packages or access to a statistician.

The incomplete block design was preferred in this study as it was felt that interval/ratio data could be more easily analysed and that differences between treatments could be examined using a variety of variables as a basis for the comparison.

'BLINDING' THE TRIAL

When the study was accepted for funding, the funding body were keen to have the element of blinding in the trial as strong as possible. This was a little problematic, but when it came to the actual trial my personal circumstances forced the design of the study.

Clearly the patient could not be blind in this project, as the five interventions selected were very different. Similarly, those applying the interventions (either the ward nurses or the patients themselves) could not be blind for the same reason. However, at the time of designing the study there seemed to be some scope for those involved in evaluating the areas being kept unaware of which treatments the patient was having. It was quite simple to keep the microbiologist in the dark as to the origins of each specimen in terms of which cell on the grid the patient occupied.

Blinding the researcher was more difficult; however, finally a design was arrived at in which one researcher would enter patients into the trial and the other would do the evaluations at two, seven, 14 and 28 days. The idea was that the second researcher would arrive on the ward before the patient had washed and would not see the patient until a nurse had removed all signs of the interventions in use from the patient's skin. I am still doubtful as to how effective this approach would have been, as in the actual experiment the nurses tended to put reminders on the patient's clipboards and toiletries to ensure that they remembered which intervention to put where, or they were even laid out on marked trays for left and right. Also, even if the nurses didn't reveal information to the evaluator, then often the patients would have done so by attempting to discuss the interventions with her. It is also true that where a patient was randomized to the hydrocolloid patch it left a distinctive mark on the subject's skin.

In the end the problem was taken out of my hands as the ward I was working on at the beginning of the trial had been closed and I was working in the School of Nursing whilst looking for a clinical appointment. When a post came up just as the trial was about to begin I had to take the opportunity, but unfortunately this post was 25 miles from where my research associate was working, making any chance of us both being able to see the patients in the pattern planned impossible. Whilst this may appear to be a flaw in the design, I am convinced that any claim that the evaluator in this study was blind would have been a charade, as in the case of the leg ulcer study discussed previously (Ormiston et al., 1985).

RECRUITMENT TO THE STUDY

Probably the single most important piece of advice that should be given to a an inexperienced researcher who is about to embark on a quantitative study is to consult a statistician when the project is being designed. One reason for this is that it is only by doing this that the investigator can be certain that the data which will be generated can be adequately analysed. The second reason is that if an experiment is being planned, the use of power analysis will allow the statistician to estimate how large a sample is required if a false conclusion that no relationship exists between the variables (a Type II error) is to be avoided.

Unfortunately, power analysis relies on having some estimation of the degree of change one might expect in the dependant variable. In my study this was not possible as there was no previous research in the subject, so the old method of simply trying to recruit as many subjects as possible was adopted.

Previous studies

I now know that it is remarkably common to have recruitment problems in clinical trials. Even looking at some of the research into other aspects of the breast, the literature is full of reports of recruitment difficulties. For example, in a randomized controlled study of interventions recommended by midwives for women with inverted nipples (McCandlish and Renfrew, 1991) it was hoped to recruit 600 women in one year; however after nine months only 100 had been included in the trial. Doctors have experienced similar problems. Jack *et al.* (1990) report recruitment problems in a number of studies examining treatments for breast cancer. In an overview of Scottish trials for breast cancer the rate of entry was 22.2% of those eligible to take part. In their own trial, Jack *et al.* found that only 27.2% of patients who were suitable were actually entered into one of two trials in progress at their centre. None of these quite match the difficulty experienced in the United States, where it has been suggested that only 2% of eligible patients are entered into breast cancer trials (DeVita, 1989). Clearly then, the problem of recruitment to clinical trials is common, yet it is not mentioned in any detail in nursing research texts.

Recruitment problems

I was largely unaware of the problem of recruitment to clinical trials when I commenced the experimental phase of the research. In fact I was reasonably confident that we would be able to enter about 100 patients into the study in a year to 18 months, but anticipated that only 75% of them would remain in the study for the full 28 days. I knew from the prevalence study that we had found 65 patients with active lesions on one day and even though many of these were either confused or had some other condition which would make them ineligible for the main study, I felt that the numbers were high enough that sufficient suitable patients would be forthcoming. I also knew that when we had recruited for the patient interviews, one researcher had entered 22 patients in two months; for the experimental phase there would be two of us.

The mechanism for getting patients referred was either by the researchers visiting targeted wards every week or by any ward contacting the research team via a radiopager. Yet the recruitment record for the first seven months of data collection was extremely disappointing but, it seems, not untypical. In that time 100 patients were referred to the trial, of which only 17 were entered into the study. Of those 17, three withdrew subsequently, to leave data on only 14 participants. The reasons

Table 6.1 The reasons for the failure to enter
patients into the trial from the first 100 referrals

Reason	Number
Consultant refused consent	14
Patient confused	13
Patient refused	12
Unilateral lesion	8
Patient too ill	7
Going/gone home	5
Laboratory not available	4
Patient dysphasic/aphasic	4
Lesions healed	3
Patient too distressed	3
Patient died	2
Patient too deaf	1
Not recorded	7
Total	**83**

for failure to enter the trial are summarized in Table 6.1 and
discussed in detail below.

Consultant's reticence to support the study

Because consultants are seen to be the people who are ultimately accountable for the treatment that patients receive,
research involving patients' treatments not only needs to be
passed by an ethics committee but also requires the express
consent of each patient's consultant. Many nurses would argue
that as this study relates to nursing treatment, the need for the
consultant's agreement is anachronistic. Indeed, about half of
the 60 consultants contacted did not reply at all – even to
refuse consent – to the request to involve their patients in the
study. This was despite written reminders and my making it
simple for them by providing them with a form which they
only had to tick, sign and return in the envelope provided.
Only two replied that they did not wish their patients to be
included in the experiment.

With this level of response (which I found difficult to attribute
to anything other than apathy or, sometimes, arrogance) I was
tempted to write and say that if I didn't receive a reply I would

assume that this meant that they had no objections. However, the reason that I did contact them in the first place and decided not to take silence as consent in the second was that it would only take one consultant to strongly and publicly object to this approach and I would have ruined the prospects of nurse researchers coming after me who wanted to perform research which involved treating patients.

Nonetheless it was extremely galling that often patients who were keen to take part could not be entered into the trial because their consultant apparently could not be bothered to reply to my letter. The number of referrals from wards which had patients from non-consenting consultants was kept low, of course, by the researchers not visiting those wards when looking for referrals.

Patients refusing consent

It is right, of course, that patients should enter clinical trials voluntarily; the rule in the District where this research took place being that the patient should have at least 24 hours to think about whether they should take part or not before being entered into the trial. Both my research associates and I had the experience of patients who refused to take part whom we felt that if we had 'pushed', would have consented. The issue of how persuasive one ought to be is not often discussed and this may be affected by whether one feels that the patient has a moral obligation to participate (Sim, 1991). Our experience demonstrated to us how easy it would have been with a largely elderly and vulnerable sample to, in our view, break the rules for the personal gain of having adequate numbers in the study.

Restrictive research criteria

The purpose of setting research criteria is to control variables and facilitate the research. For example, the criterion that the lesion must extend more than 3 cm onto the chest wall was a requirement if the method used to collect the microbiological specimens was to be the same for every patient. This is very much a balancing act; the more criteria that are set the better controlled the experiment but it is more difficult to find patients who fulfil them. The criteria set in this study (Table 6.2) ac-

Table 6.2 A summary of the main criteria used in selecting patients

The patient must be over 18 years of age
The patient must be able to give informed consent
The lesion must be bilateral
The patient must be well enough to participate
The patient's immune system must be working adequately
The lesion must extend at least 3 cm on to the chest wall
This must be the only pathology affecting the skin of the breasts
The patient must be able to communicate adequately

counted for at least a fifth of those who were referred not being entered. Again, this is artificially low because the researchers did not visit wards where patients were unlikely to fulfil all the criteria, for example wards for the elderly mentally ill.

Laboratory constraints

As time went on, the laboratory which was processing micro-biological specimens for us imposed more and more constraints on when they would accept them. This was never adequately overcome and the figure of only four patients not accepted because the laboratory was not available only reflects where a ward had contacted the project via the radiopager; the researchers did not visit the wards looking for patients on days when they knew that the specimens would be ignored.

The collecting of complete data on only 14 patients out of the first 100 referrals was depressing and was followed by a period of extended sickness by the research assistant. Only one complete grid was available for analysis, resulting in the decision being made that this focus of the study would be used as a pilot for the methodology, especially as other examples of this type of experimental design are extremely difficult to find in the nursing literature.

Whilst the experimental phase has generated an enormous amount of survey type data which will be useful, there is a degree of disappointment not to have a 'result' for the experiment and at times a feeling of failure. There is consolation in the realization that it is difficult to see how the problem could have been avoided; power analysis was not possible, a prevalence study was performed, there was no precedent in the

District for inviting the consent of so many consultants so the poor response from them could not have been predicted. It would have been unethical to pressure patients into taking part, reducing the research criteria would have affected the element of control in the study and the sickness of the research assistant could not have been anticipated. There is also consolation in sharing the experience with others who may embark on experimental research, especially when it would seem that other studies by researchers more experienced than myself have had similar difficulties.

CONCLUSION

This chapter has described some of the experiences of performing an experiment. The point was made that it is essential to perform the necessary exploratory work before embarking on the trial, no matter how tempting it may be to press on with trying to support or reject a hypothesis. The desire to test several interventions was not as problematic methodologically as is popularly believed; however, introducing the component of blinding into nursing research is possibly more difficult. In this study, recruitment to the trial became a major issue. It is at this point, when the researcher begins to see his or her project running into difficulty, that I believe the elements of rigour and ethical conduct in the design of the study must be strictly upheld, at the cost of the project if necessary.

I feel that the experiment is neither a more nor a less difficult method of research to implement than other research methods. It does not deserve the mystique which often seems to surround it, but as with any research method it must be carefully planned and implemented. If at the conclusion of the project the number of subjects included does not result in a hypothesis being supported, then equally the hypothesis should not be rejected as this conclusion cannot be supported either; to do so would be a case of trial and (Type II) error.

REFERENCES

Bagenal, F., Easton, D., Harris, E., Chilvers, C., and McElwain, T. (1990) Survival of patients with breast cancer attending Bristol Cancer Help Centre. *The Lancet*, **336**, 606–10.

Carlisle, D. (1991) Research stopped at Bristol Cancer Centre (news item). *Nursing Times*, **87**(49), 8.

Cook-Mozaffari, P., Darby, S., and Doll, R. (1989) Cancer near potential sites of nuclear installations. *The Lancet*, **2**(8672), 1145–7.

Corner, J. (1991) In search of more complete answers to research questions. Quantitative versus qualitative research methods: is there a way forward? *Journal of Advanced Nursing*, **16**(6), 718–28.

DeVita, V.T. (1989) Breast cancer therapy: exercising all our options. *New England Journal of Medicine*, **320**, 527–9.

Dumas, R. (1987) Clinical trials in nursing. *Recent Advances in Nursing*, **1**(17), 108–25.

Editorial (1948) The controlled therapeutic trial. *British Medical Journal*, **ii**, 791–2.

Forman, D., Cook-Mozaffari, P., and Darby, S. (1987) Cancer near nuclear installations. *Nature*, **329**, 499–505.

Jack, W.J.L., Chetty, U., and Rodger, A. (1990) Recruitment to a prospective breast conservation trial: why are so few patients randomized? *British Medical Journal*, **301**, 83–5.

McCandlish, R. and Renfrew, M. (1991) Trial and tribulation. *Nursing Times*, **87**(38), 40–1.

McMahon, R. (1991) The prevalence of skin problems beneath the breasts of in-patients. *Nursing Times (occasional paper)*, **87**(39), 48–51.

Medical Research Council (1948) Streptomycin treatment of pulmonary tuberculosis. *British Medical Journal*, **ii**, 767–82.

Murray, Y. (1988) Tradition rather than cure? *Nursing Times*, **84**(38), 75–80.

Ormiston, M., Seymour, M., Venn, G., Cohen, R., and Fox, J. (1985) Controlled trial of Iodosorb in chronic venous ulcers. *British Medical Journal*, **291**, 308–10.

Polit, D. and Hungler, B. (1987) *Nursing Research: Principles and Methods*, 3rd edn, Lippincott, Philadelphia.

Sim, J. (1991) Nursing research: is there an obligation on subjects to participate? *Journal of Advanced Nursing*, **16**(11), 1284–9.

Sleep, J. and Grant, A. (1988) Effects of salt and Savlon bath concentrate post-partum. *Nursing Times (occasional paper)*, **84**(21), 55–7.

7

Interviewing carers in their own homes

Jill Buckeldee

Interviewing is rather like marriage: everybody knows what it is, an awful lot of people do it, and yet behind each closed door is a world of secrets.

(Oakley, 1981)

INTRODUCTION

This chapter explores my personal experiences of conducting unstructured interviews with carers[†] in their own homes.

As part of an MSc in Nursing I undertook a project examining district nurses'[*] work with carers in the community (Buckeldee, 1989). Since this project was exploring new territory a potential method of collecting some of the data appeared to be by conducting unstructured interviews with carers. However at that time I failed to appreciate the highly complex skills and numerous considerations essential for embarking on such a venture. Such details are rarely mentioned in research texts, despite Oakley's observation in 1981 and yet it is a common research method.

It is in order to help to rectify this omission that my account of undertaking unstructured interviews, highlighting the problems encountered, is being recounted here. My continued involvement in interviewing carers confirms my belief that

---

[†] A carer is a person who provides care to a client (physically, psychologically/emotionally and/or socially) for no financial gain.
[*] A district nurse visits clients in their own homes. S/he is a trained nurse who has undergone additional training to obtain a district nursing qualification.

much learning about, and experience of, using this research method is required in order for it to be a truly fruitful form of data collection. First though, some background and detail about the study will be given.

BACKGROUND TO THE STUDY

The initial idea for this project arose from my practice as a district nurse and from talks with the supervisor of the project. In practice I had observed that some clients regularly received less help from community nurses simply because a carer was present and seemingly regardless of the carer's needs. Whilst recognizing that at times it is appropriate to provide minimal support for carers in order to enable them to continue caring for their relative/friend, I was aware of the growing wealth of literature demonstrating the stress, strain, burdens and financial costs that many carers experience, e.g. Gilleard *et al.* (1984), George and Gwyther (1986), Whittick (1988). Also I was aware that district nurses are supposed to be trained to work effectively with carers (National Boards, 1986).

However, confounding this issue for some district nurses is the perceived lack of resources to enable them to undertake their work effectively combined with the seemingly increasing numbers of clients in the community.

A review of the literature revealed very little work exploring district nurses' work with carers. Only two studies were found which included this topic within them (Hudson and Hawthorne, 1988; Luker and Perkins, 1988). Since little appeared to be known about how district nurses manage this aspect of their work I eventually decided to focus on the question:

What happens when district nurses visit clients who are cared for by a carer?

Another aspect which might have been examined is the processes by which district nurses are referred clients with carers and how nurses reach a decision whether to visit them. However the fact that the project had to be completed in one year, since it was part of a part time Master of Science in Nursing, was a major constraining factor and hence the former aspect was chosen. Resultant exploratory work led to the following aims for the study:

1. To determine the focus of the nurse's visits through observations and recordings of the caring setting and examination of the client/carer records.
2. To identify patterns of verbal interaction in the caring setting by tape recording all interactions.
3. To identify the carer's role and actions during nurse visits by observing the caring setting.
4. To elicit carers' views about the problems they experience in their role and the help they receive and would like to receive from formal services.

In this discussion I will be mainly focusing on the method used to fulfil aim 4.

At the time of the project I was a practising district nurse which proved very helpful in that the networks for approaching participants and gaining ethical approval were well known to me and undoubtedly facilitated the project. However, potentially constraining the project was my relative novice status in terms of undertaking unstructured interviews.

I chose this method since it provides a description of situations with information obtained in the participant's own words and not with the researcher's views imposed on them and I felt that this was most appropriate to fulfil the research aims.

Swanson (1986, p. 67) argues that in an unstructured formal interview the interviewer may use an interview guide containing a set of brief, general questions or a topic outline and that it is particularly helpful to the interviewer new to this type of interviewing. I used an interview guide mainly to reassure me that general areas that I intended to discuss in the interview were in fact covered.

The setting, some of the skills and the approach required for performing unstructured interviews are detailed in research texts, e.g. Chenitz and Swanson (1986), Field and Morse (1985). Having read such texts, I was aware of the need for the interviewer to be free from anxiety about her/himself, which appeared a tall order, indeed enough to cause anxiety in itself! Still, my background in nursing and my albeit limited skills in interviewing nurses as an undergraduate student at least gave me a base from which to start. The following is an account of my experiences in this field.

THE SETTING FOR THE INTERVIEWS

Although Swanson (1986, p. 71) argues that much can be gained by interviewing couples as a unit since two responses are gained instead of one and that one person may clarify the other's perception of an event, I decided to interview the carer alone. This was principally because the carers of clients were the focus of the study and it was their views that were sought. Further, I felt that the clients may in some cases inhibit the carers' expression of feelings, particularly if they were feeling burdened or stressed by their situation, as much of the literature seemed to indicate.

Perhaps rather naively I anticipated that there would be few problems in ensuring that the carer was interviewed alone with me. I was wrong. In one case in particular, one male patient insisted that his wife, who was his carer, would talk with me only in his presence. As the interview progressed it became only too apparent that the carer was extremely inhibited in her responses. Of course this could have been because of my limited skills as an interviewer; however I did not believe this to be the case since I had already conducted some interviews and had not had any problems in encouraging carers to talk. Furthermore, on my first visit to arrange the interview, the carer in question had been alone in the house and had talked freely with me. The client's influence was further felt when towards the end of the interview he even began to answer for his wife! Such interruptions continued despite my pleas.

Although the situation itself was illuminating it did little towards obtaining an account of the carer's views. I felt very angry about the client interruptions and at that precise moment I really did not know what to do. Rather lamely I continued the sham of the 'interview'. With hindsight, I should have anticipated that this could happen and if possible arranged the interview when the client was out. This would certainly have prevented placing the carer and myself in such a difficult situation.

Although it was a painful experience it highlighted the importance of establishing exactly where an interview will take place and the need to ensure that it is free from distraction prior to the interview.

THE WILLINGNESS OF CARERS TO TALK

Although I had some experience of interviewing clients I still felt some apprehension about this method of data collection. I had read many research texts about the skills required but I still had some doubts about whether I could get information from carers. Could I establish relationships with carers so they did not feel threatened but could tell me about the world from their own point of view?

My fears dissipated during the exploratory study when it became apparent that carers were only too willing to make time to talk with me, often about very personal matters and frequently for much longer periods than I had anticipated. I often spent between one and two hours with them. Although I was pleased with this it also raised some concerns.

First, although I spoke with carers several times before the interviews, to request their participation in the study and then to arrange the interview, few of them asked questions about the study or about the confidentiality of the material. Being known by their district nurse provided some confirmation of my identity. I found it extremely easy to get carers to agree to take part in the project, mirroring Finch's (1984, p. 73) experiences of interviewing women. For this reason interviewees need to know how to protect themselves from researchers. Interestingly, Finch (1984, p. 80) argues that it was principally her status and demeanour as a woman rather than anything to do with the research process that caused women to place their trust in her. Finch felt that any woman could offer assurances and be believed. I experienced such trust with both male and female carers. The effectiveness of young female interviewers has been noted elsewhere (Dingwell, 1980; Wax, 1971).

Still, there is an exploitative potential in such trust making people vulnerable as subjects of research. Following on from Finch's (1984, p. 83) argument people should know what is going to happen to the data. Most carers in my study could not have been absolutely sure what was going to happen to the information so readily given. More importantly, it was unlikely that they would profit directly from the study, certainly not in the short term. The information that they gave could potentially have been used to support arguments that they may have disagreed with. This stresses the importance of the informed consent procedure, highlighting that such a procedure is designed to protect subjects from exploitation and any possible damage.

A second point for consideration was that the ease with which carers talked with me was startling. Like others, e.g. Finch (1984, p. 72) and Binnie (1988), I had expected to have to work very hard to encourage participants to speak freely with me. Clearly this was not the case. Carers apparently welcomed the opportunity to talk about themselves and many of the interviews took the form of an intimate conversation (Finch, 1984, p. 73). Many participants did not often have the time and/or the opportunity to sit and talk and it may have been that they took advantage of this situation. Others rarely saw other people and so also may have used this opportunity to simply socialize. Still, frequently I felt that I was being treated as a confidant, as someone who understood, and consequently information about their caring experiences was obtained often with minimal effort.

The readiness of many carers to talk also brought with it the practical problem of encouraging talk and yet ensuring that it was broadly concerned with my study. At times participants became immersed in long and detailed stories of their lives which apparently bore no relevance to my study. As a relatively novice interviewer I found it very difficult to guide participants back onto the broad aims of the interview. I was unsure when this needed to be done – at the end of stories or accounts or during them? At times I felt extremely uncomfortable during interviews, particularly when a carer had been talking for quite a while, knowing what I should do in terms of redirecting the conversation but not being sure how to do so.

Further complicating matters was the issue of being able to determine what is useful and what isn't when undertaking unstructured interviews. I was unsure whether I could tell at this stage of the study. For some topics of conversation their irrelevance was obvious; for example, I had conversations about the weather and climatic changes over the years and television programmes and the nature of programming today.

However, for other topics of conversation it was not so clear, e.g. accounts of carers' and clients' family history. I erred on the side of caution and encouraged talk if I was not sure how relevant and informative it was, even if it did mean interviews lasting over an hour.

Transcribing and preliminary coding of early interviews helped in several ways. First it gave me feedback about my interviewing skills (or lack of them at times!) which proved invaluable. It also helped to identify areas requiring further exploration which in turn helped to direct later interviews. Furthermore as the interviews progressed my own confidence and skill in conducting interviews increased and was verifed in later transcripts of interviews.

With hindsight, practice in conducting such interviews with peers or other researchers would have been helpful for, as so often happens in nursing, despite wide reading on the topic it was only through experience that my skills developed.

IDENTIFICATION OF NEW FEELINGS

As mentioned previously, not only did most carers willingly talk with me but many also freely talked about themselves, including personal and intimate matters. At times this process also resulted in participants exploring new feelings and ideas that they had not previously considered or acknowledged. This commonly occurred when we explored their feelings and perceptions of their caring role. The depth of sorrow and sadness that I felt at such times was almost overwhelming. I was not sure of my responsibilities to these people. Having 'got my data' I did not know whether I should leave the carers in the hope that they would solve or deal with their problems in their own way or whether, having caused them to realize feelings not previously acknowledged, I had a responsibility to help them in some way. If the latter was the case I needed to know what the nature of that responsibility was.

I was deeply concerned and very confused on this point and questioned the value of helping carers to realize some of their feelings just for my study. Swanson (1986, p. 68) warns that wearing the nurse's hat versus the researcher's hat may be problematic to the novice researcher and I took her advice and spent some time with the participants following the interview, talking with them and answering any questions or queries that they had. This may have been helpful for them as at this point carers often continued talking about what they had said during the interview.

This dilemma was also helped by talking with my peers and colleagues and agreeing that, subject to the carer's approval, for confidentiality had been guaranteed, any pressing problems which they wanted help with would be reported to the appropriate nurse/person. This was probably more reassuring for me than the relevant carer for some stated that they did not feel that the nurse could help them anyway.

I still experience some concern about this and it reinforces the need to ensure that the intentions of a project and its potential for confirming/generating new knowledge are fully considered by researchers and ethical committees, including the potential effects on participants. More importantly such effects on participants need to be reduced to an absolute minimum and the potential for such effects should be communicated to possible new participants.

THERAPEUTIC EFFECTS OF INTERVIEWING

Despite such problems, I also felt, and indeed some carers stated, that there were therapeutic effects for them as a result of participating in the interviews. Many carers readily expressed their feelings about their caring role and their living arrangements. Most of them explained why they were in a caring role and many talked about there not being an option about this, emphasizing that they felt a sense of duty to their role, as demonstrated by the comment from one carer:

> I'm his wife, what else can I do? I couldn't let anyone else look after him.

There appeared to be a confirmation and/or an acceptance, albeit relunctantly at times, of the caring role. Although some participants were obviously not happy in their role there was also an acceptance that they would not want things any other way. For such carers there was a sense of resignation about their situation, reaffirming and making sense of their position. On a personal level I found this difficult to deal with at times. For others, the interview provided a vehicle for the carer to reaffirm his/her feelings for the client. There appeared to be a feeling for some that, despite the difficulties inherent in their domestic situation, they still loved and cared deeply for the client. For others talking about their situation appeared to allow a restructuring of it, helping to regain some sense of their position.

Whatever the carer's feelings about the client and the caring role, the interview also provided an opportunity for participants to literally have a moan about their lives, giving them an opportunity to verbalize their feelings. I asked each carer how they felt about their caring role and this typically produced an expression of deep feelings. At such points I merely listened while they spoke, frequently for lengthy periods of time, about their day-to-day difficulties and their feelings about this. The cathartic value of this was stated by several participants following the interview.

The giving of time just for the carer and the signs of interest and understanding that I conveyed when with them were apparently something rarely shown to them even by close friends and family. Many participants stated that they were very lonely. Some carers clearly relished such time, exploiting the opportunity to talk about themselves. Such findings were also found in Finch's (1984) study of clergymens' wives and women involved in preschool playgroups and also in Oakley's (1979) study of the transition to motherhood. Oakley's identification of the need for a therapeutic listener for mothers outside of family and friends could thus be extended to carers of dependent people in the community.

A final therapeutic effect of the interviews was the feeling of helping other carers and carers of the future by taking part in the study. Some participants stated that the principal reason for taking part in the study was that it would hopefully help other carers. They were keen to do this since they knew what caring for someone at home was like and that if it would help someone in any way then participation was justified.

THE RECORDING OF THE INTERVIEWS

From the outset I decided to tape record the interviews in order to allow me to concentrate on them and to ensure that the information obtained was accurately recorded. A Sony tape cassette recorder (TCM-12) was used which had a built-in microphone, thus ensuring that there was one less gadget to be concerned about.

Obtaining either no recording or inaudible recordings during the exploratory phase of the study highlighted the need for me to practise in this area. In some instances the batteries were not working, the volume had been set too low, there was background noise from a radio or TV or I forgot to press the record button! The sheer frustration that I experienced when this happened cannot be described but it did ensure that I practised using the recorder. Further, I did not want to be distracted by it during the visit or for any anxieties about it to be reflected in my interviewing skills. Thus before each visit I ensured that the recorder was working and set the volume. I changed the batteries frequently, usually after two interviews. I knew that I was being cautious, even neurotic, but I did not want to risk the interview not being recorded. I had decided against using a tape recorder with a plug since I did not want to be confined to places near a socket.

The need to place the recorder between myself and the participant was learnt early on when one tape produced a wonderful recording of my voice but a very muffled recording of the participant.

Initially I was unsure what length of tape to use. The first interviews were between 45 and 90 minutes, so C30s were no good. I felt that I would be taking a risk with C120s since they are thin and fragile and often break. Thus C90s were used, with no problems, and extra tapes were carried in case interviews lasted over 90 minutes.

It is advisable to have a recorder that informs you when the tape has ended, for a couple of times in the initial interviews I was not immediately aware of this and thus lost a small amount of data before I realized that the tape needed turning over.

The quality and volume of the data obtained demonstrated that the recorder did not seem to inhibit carers in their talk.

LEAVING THE CARER'S HOUSE

My inexperience of undertaking unstructured interviews was exemplified in my feelings of uncertainty about when to leave the carer's house. Despite making it very clear that an interview had finished, by stating that it had and by obviously turning off the tape recorder, most carers continued to talk. Frequently, conversation was reaffirming the content of the interview (Hobson, 1978). Also many carers seemed to be enjoying the conversation, initiating most of it.

Particularly in the early interviews my feelings were that, having helped me with my study, it was only fair to spend time talking with participants if they wanted this. However at times when it felt that some carers possibly might never stop talking, it was difficult to know how to handle the situation. With hindsight it would probably have been better to be honest and repeat that I had finished the visit and to ask if there were any more questions or queries before I left. Clearly this would not be recommended immediately after the interview has finished but after some social conversation.

Many carers demonstrated great expertise in encouraging me to stay by either introducing new topics of detailed conversation and/or offering beverages, perhaps further emphasizing the need for a 'therapeutic listener'.

I felt that my skills in this improved as I undertook more interviews and I began instinctively to feel the right time to prepare for exiting from a carer's home.

EXHAUSTION

Undertaking such interviews can be very tiring and completing each interview frequently left me exhausted. Because I had to travel over 50 miles to reach my sample I arranged to interview two carers on the same day. This proved to be the maximum possible for me and is recognized as the optimum number to prevent overload (Swanson, 1986, p. 72).

By becoming immersed in the interview, genuinely interested and alert, a great deal of energy was required particularly if I wanted to respond to cues and to remain aware of what had and was being said. Empathizing and sympathizing with carers' feelings added to my feelings of tiredness.

At times interviewing two carers per day seemed too much, particularly when I was still transcribing previous interviews. Ideally each interview needed to be transcribed shortly after it had taken place but at times this was impossible due to time constraints. Notably some of the earlier interviews were not transcribed until 5–7 days after they had taken place. Clearly timing of interviews to allow transcription was helpful. Feelings of exhaustion did lessen over time as my skills in interviewing developed and my effectiveness in dealing with carers' feelings increased.

CONCLUSIONS

This chapter highlights the complex skills and numerous considerations required for conducting unstructured interviews. I rather simplistically assumed that interviewing carers would provide a reasonably easy method for achieving some of my research aims. However it proved to be a messy process which required involvement with carers' feelings and empathy with their problems.

Practice is recommended for those embarking on such a method and feedback on one's skills should be sought by giving tapes or transcripts to someone familiar with this method who can critically evaluate the interviewing skills used. There is a need for projects to be appropriately supervised and thus enable the researchers to be adequately supported. Further the potential for a project to generate and/or validate new knowledge must be ensured in order for ethical approval to be granted. With such preparation a great wealth of data is likely to be generated.

REFERENCES

Binnie, A. (1988) Working lives of staff nurses: a sociological perspective. University of Warwick. MA dissertation.

Buckeldee, J.M. (1989) A preliminary analysis of the role and interactions of the district nurse with lay carers in the community. King's College, London. MSc dissertation.

Chenitz, W. and Swanson, J. (1986) *From Practice to Grounded Theory*, Addison-Wesley, California.

Dingwall, R. (1980) Ethics and ethnography. *Sociological Review*, **28**(4), 871–91.

Field, P. and Morse, J. (1985) *Nursing Research. The Application of Qualitative Approaches*, Croom Helm, London.

Finch, J. (1984) 'It's great to have someone to talk to': the ethics and politics of interviewing, in *Social Researching. Politics, Problems, Practice*, (eds C. Bell and H. Roberts), Routledge and Kegan Paul, London.

George, L.K., and Gwyther, L.P. (1986) Caregiver well-being. A multidimensional examination of family caregivers of demented adults. *The Gerontologist*, **26**, 253–9.

Gilleard, C.J., Gilleard, E., Gledhill, K., and Whittick, J. (1984) Caring for the elderly mentally infirm at home: a survey of the supporters. *Journal of Epidemiology and Community Health*, **38**, 319–25.

Hobson, D. (1978) Housewives; isolation as oppression, in *Women Take Issue: Aspects of Women's Subordination*, Women's Study Group, Centre for Contemporary Cultural Studies, Hutchinson, London.

Hudson, M. and Hawthorne, P. (1988) Stroke patients in the community. *Nursing Times*, **84**(5), 51.

Luker, K. and Perkins, E. (1988) Lay carers' views on the district nursing service. *Midwife, Health Visitor and Community Nurse*, **24**(4), 132–4.

National Boards for England, Wales, Scotland and Northern Ireland (1986) *Curriculum. District Nursing for Registered General Nurses*, Bocardo Press, Oxford.

Oakley, A. (1979) *Becoming a Mother*, Martin Robertson, Oxford.

Oakley, A. (1981) Interviewing women: a contradiction in terms, in *Doing Feminist Research*, (ed. H. Roberts), Routledge and Kegan Paul, London.

Swanson, J. (1986) The formal qualitative interview for grounded theory, in *From Practice to Grounded Theory*, (eds W. Chenitz and J. Swanson), Addison-Wesley, California.

Wax, R. (1971) *Doing Fieldwork*, University of Chicago Press, Chicago.

Whittick, J.E. (1988) Dementia and mental handicap: emotional distress in carers. *British Journal of Clinical Psychology*, **27**, 167–72.

8

Experiences of method triangulation

Ann Bergen

BEGINNINGS

My induction into the research experience has left me with a rather cynical suspicion that as much in the business happens by chance as by design. Certainly this proved to be the case with the genesis of my project although I could, in retrospect, flatter myself that I had a heightened sensitivity to opportunistic circumstances.

The project was a course requirement. The subject matter and methodology were matters for 'the future' but our team of three Macmillan (continuing care) nurses*, having recently established itself, was being 'encouraged' to evaluate its role. The nature of their workload at the time made the suggestion less than feasible. So they thought of me.

The idea of looking at the Macmillan nurse's role grew on me. Caring for terminally ill people in the community was an aspect of the district nursing work that I was then involved in which gave me much satisfaction and an opportunity, it seemed, to use all my nursing skills. I agreed, almost by default, to undertake the evaluation.

Choice of research approach seemed similarly to arise initially from circumstance rather than any epistemological or methodological preferences. This was just as well. A remit of 'evalu-

---

* A Macmillan or continuing care nurse is a registered general nurse with an additional district nursing or health visiting qualification and a specific expertise in care of the dying. Of the three nurses participating in the study, two were sponsored by Cancer Relief Macmillan Fund and one employed by the health authority.

ation' in any context was enough to make even a novice researcher like me realize that the proverbial can of worms would sooner or later manifest itself as several complex issues needing to be addressed: what constituted value? whose evaluation would be measured? what about reliability and validity?

The health authority in which I worked had recently initiated a Standard Setting programme and a Standard on Care of the Dying was being drafted as a working statement by practitioners (including district and continuing care nurses) of the criteria they felt must be met in order to provide an agreed level of nursing care. Therein lay part of the solution to my questions. Value could be seen in terms of meeting a certain standard within a needs based framework; it could be stated from the nursing viewpoint (and, after all, nurses are in the best position to state what good nursing is, aren't they?); and the Standard's criteria could form the basis of a useful interview schedule for someone with no experience of constructing such tools.

It all seemed very logical. It was also, as I soon discovered, rather a simplistic way of looking at research. But it was a beginning and it gave me a framework within which to think out more systematically my aims, theoretical stance and methodological issues such as reliability and validity.

METHODOLOGICAL ISSUES

The problem – quantitative *v.* qualitative

Much of the debate surrounding research, both in nursing and more generally, has converged on the quantitative–quanlitative debate. The received view has tended to present the two approaches as mutually exclusive paradigms representing divergent views about the way in which social reality ought to be studied (Bryman, 1988). Quantitative research has been presented as the means of testing existing theories deductively (through hypothesis construction), while qualitative designs have become accepted as the mode through which theories may be generated inductively from the data. The method of choice should, in theory, become obvious once a research question has been stated and be based on factors such as the amount of existing knowledge in the given field.

Thinking through these issues certainly helped me to refine my own ideas for conducting my project. The literature review had yielded some useful findings regarding nursing care of the terminally ill in the community, though it tended to be process rather than outcome based and from a nurse rather than patient perspective. In addition, some research tools were identified as capable of 'quantifying' (on a numerical basis) concepts such as quality of life and levels of distress among cancer patients. It seemed to me that I could use this work by:

- predicting certain outcomes with regard to the nursing care of the patients I was looking at (by establishing 'hypotheses');
- using categories derived from the literature, as well as the Standard criteria, to ensure that I covered the ground adequately within my subject area;
- standardizing the interview format across the two groups of nurses involved (district and continuing care nurses);
- creating a data collection tool which would facilitate the analysis.

Yet, there was more to it than this. The whole issue of quality of care as I had conceived it lacked a crucial dimension, a point not easily lost on my course tutor who, to my eternal gratitude, unrelentingly pursued the issue until I saw the light. The dimension was, of course, that of the 'consumer' of care, the patient. I suppose my reluctance to take this on board was the unease I felt about the prospect of talking to very frail and ill people in their homes; it occurred to me as a rather unnecessary intrusion into their precarious existence. But it did make sense. The advantage conferred on the quality of the data by an account direct from those for whom the service being studied exists would be considerable.

However, this inclusion would necessitate a rethink *vis à vis* methodology. The 'consumers' whose views I aimed to elicit would not have been involved in establishing the criteria for care and I felt that such a checklist approach (based on items selected by others) would be constraining. I wanted to know what *they*, as individuals, focused on within the nurse–patient scenario, as much as what they felt about pre-existing para-meters. Further, there was the possibility of the well-documented 'positive set bias' (French, 1981) whereby patients tend indiscriminately to express satisfaction when asked about the quality of care. So, while I still felt the need to incorporate the benefits, listed above, of a 'quantitative' approach, I also felt the need for an 'emic' viewpoint, the need to access the feelings, opinions and preoccupations which my respondents owned themselves, particularly the patient group.

The solution – triangulation

Nursing has not been the only discipline to challenge the discreteness of the two 'ideal type' approaches to research adopted by the purists. Indeed, Bell and Roberts, in the field of sociology, describe the latter's account of 'doing sociological research' in the 1970s as reflecting upon 'the break up of what is referred to as the hegemony of positivistic epistemology' (Bell and Roberts, 1984, p. 5). They document the emergence of 'decent methodological pluralism', which sanctioned the grafting of a certain eclecticism onto a predefined methodological position.

The practice of combining both quantitative and qualitative data within a single study has subsequently been promoted in a variety of authoritative texts, albeit under different guises. Denzin (1978), for instance, describes 'methodological triangulation' (amongst other varieties of the concept), while Yin (1989) recommends 'multiple sources of evidence' facilitating 'convergent lines of enquiry' in order to maximize construct validity within case study research. The arguments seemed plausible to me, given that I did not want to let go of either approach and I was particularly attracted by the idea of 'convergence on truth' (Polit and Hungler, 1987, p. 332) and on the conceptual proximity of triangulation to means of estimating validity (ibid.).

My methodology, therefore, took the form outlined in Figure 8.1. I felt that the case study approach, as outlined by Yin, was particularly appropriate for the aim and subject matter of my research, which crystallized around the question illustrated at the centre of the diagram. Semi-structured interview schedules, based on the criteria of the Standard on Care of the Dying, were administered to the three respondent groups, maintaining the parameters of care but allowing some freedom of expression (including open questions). Additionally, a validated Symptom

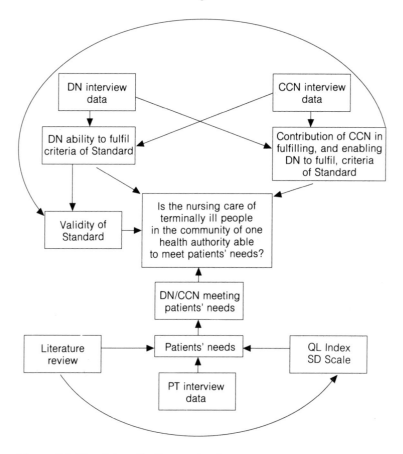

Figure 8.1 The data collection protocol
Key: DN=district nurse, CCN-continuing care nurse, PT=patient

Distress Scale (McCorkle and Young, 1978) and a Quality of Life Index (Spitzer *et al.*, 1981) were administered to the patients in order to yield some objective, quantifiable data. The degree of validity of the Standard was initially established through a process of comparing multiple sources of evidence, along the same lines of logic as was applied to the interview schedules.

Thus, in theory, all was set up. Data from the multiple sources, using different methods, would converge to answer the question regarding the quality of care of this client group within this particular setting.

CONTRADICTIONS

It hardly occurred to me that the 'lines of enquiry' might not converge. At least, I half expected some mismatch between what the patients expressed about their needs and care and what the nurses thought. The literature review had steered me away from that degree of naivety. But what did come as an initially inexplicable conundrum was that the data produced from the two types of interview with one respondent seemed in some cases to point in *divergent* directions! I therefore intend to focus on very specific elements of the research project – the semi-structured interview and Symptom Distress Scale as directed to the patient sample – in order to discuss the research-in-practice dilemma which confronted me and how, with hindsight, I could offer possible explanations for its occurrence.

Firstly, the nature of the instruments needs to be explored. The interview schedule (Figure 8.2.), as discussed, was based on the process criteria detailed in the Standard on Care of the Dying set by nurses. This, in turn, was based on the health authority's needs based philosophy of care enshrined in a written mission statement. It can be seen that the overall aim with regard to any topic was to establish whether the patient could identify any problem related to it, whether it had been discussed with either nurse attending (district or continuing care nurse) and whether this had helped. However, this explicit aim was also a launching pad from which the patient could explore, in their own time and words, the extent, nature and meaning of these problems in their own way. The open questions at the end were attempts to tap 'extras' with regard to the universe of problems which may have been helped by the nurses and also 'omissions' – problems overlooked by the nurses or, in other words, negative aspects of care.

The Symptom Distress Scale (SDS – McCorkle and Young, 1978; Figure 8.3.), in contrast, is a very structured tool consisting of ten symptoms with corresponding statements relating to their two extremes, separated by a scale 5 to 1 (maximum to minimum). The respondent is asked to indicate which number most closely resembles how they currently feel. The scale was tested for reliability and validity in two pilot studies by the authors with cancer patients and is based on symptoms identified by patients as being important to them. Where

Patient No: *Date:*

I am carrying out a project which is looking at the needs felt by people at home, which the district nurse or continuing care nurse might be able to help with. I would be grateful if you could assist me with this.

If I suggest a few topics, perhaps you could tell me if you have had a problem or need related to it, whether you have discussed this with any nurse, and if (s)he has been able to help.

I would like to assure you that anything you tell me will be treated in confidence.

Topic	Problem	Discussed	Helped
Pain problems	Y/N	DN/CCN	Y/N
Appetite (eating/drinking problems)	Y/N	DN/CCN	Y/N
Problems with waterworks or bowels	Y/N	DN/CCN	Y/N
Other physical symptoms (e.g. sickness, sleeplessness, tiredness, getting about, cough, breathing, wounds/sores)	Y/N	DN/CCN	Y/N
Need for any aids/equipment (e.g. bath, toilet, pressure relief aids)	Y/N	DN/CCN	Y/N
Worries related to how illness may be affecting your usual way of life	Y/N	DN/CCN	Y/N
Need for advice/information on coping with treatment, drugs or illness	Y/N	DN/CCN	Y/N
Need for any help from other services (e.g. social services, hospice, Marie Curie)	Y/N	DN/CCN	Y/N
Needs related to religious practices	Y/N	DN/CCN	Y/N
Problems or needs related to finance	Y/N	DN/CCN	Y/N

Did the district nurse discuss with you (and carer(s) if relevant) any plan for helping with any problems you mentioned to her, including helping you decide what sort of nursing and other help you want, when and where?   Y/N

Are there any other ways in which the nurses have helped?   Y/N

Can you think of any other problems/needs which you (and carer(s)) have that the nurses haven't discussed or helped with?   Y/N

Thank you for your help.

Figure 8.2 Patient interview.

Name: *Date:*

Please read the following two columns of statements, which represent opposite extremes of the symptom indicated. Then circle the number on the scale 1–5 which most closely resembles how you feel today.

Symptom	Degrees of distress	
Nausea As sick as I possibly could feel	5 4 3 2 1	I do not feel sick at all
Mood Could not feel more miserable	5 4 3 2 1	Could not feel happier
Appetite Can't face food at all	5 4 3 2 1	Normal appetite
Insomnia Couldn't have been worse	5 4 3 2 1	A perfect night
Pain Worst pain I have ever had	5 4 3 2 1	No pain
Mobility Not able to get around	5 4 3 2 1	Able to do everything
Fatigue Could not feel more tired	5 4 3 2 1	I am not tired at all
Bowel pattern The worst I've ever had	5 4 3 2 1	Normal bowel pattern
Concentration Cannot concentrate at all	5 4 3 2 1	Normal concentration
Appearance The worst I've ever felt	5 4 3 2 1	Appearance has not changed
	Score:	

Figure 8.3 Symptom distress scale.

•patients were unable to fill the form in unaided, I assisted with reading and marking the scale.

The scale was administered following the interview and was intended to supplement earlier data by actually attempting to quantify (albeit subjectively) the significance of any symptom. In practice the instruments frequently yielded not supplementary but discrete data which could not easily be reconciled with the alternative data source. This manifested itself in one of three ways:

1. Instances where high scoring (i.e. 4–5) symptoms on the SDS were not mentioned at interview. For instance one

patient scored 5 for distress related to appetite and appearance and 4 for distress related to mobility and fatigue. Yet none of these problems had been highlighted in the previous discussion. Another patient scored 5 in relation to sleeping difficulties and 4 in relation to mobility. Yet again, this was the only context in which these issues arose. My question was why such obviously significant concerns were not picked up at the interview stage.

2. Instances where problems mentioned at interview were not identified on the SDS. This issue was partly explained by the 'limited list' format of the Scale and was, indeed, why a supplementary interview was considered desirable (though even this had implications with regard to the validity of the instrument, particularly when three of my patients expressed considerable distress related to breathing, a problem specifically omitted by McCorkle and Young). But there did occur occasions where symptoms appearing on the Scale were scored at 1 (no problem), despite having been mentioned at interview. Problems of sickness, tiredness, forgetfulness and bowel difficulties were variously highlighted by different patients in this way.

3. Instances where low scoring (but above 1) items on the SDS were not mentioned at interview. This may be considered a lesser problem than those above, but on a five-point scale one would imagine that a score of 2 or 3 would designate a symptom as being sufficiently distracting to be spontaneously mentioned in an exercise designed to probe for such concerns. Problems related to mood, concentration and appearance were noticeably manifested in this way. This again posed validity related questions with regard to both means of data collection.

In addition, an interesting though not actually contradictory point came to light. This was the contrast between the nature of symptoms with high frequency (but not necessarily high rating) scores – such as pain and constipation – and those with lower frequency (but often high rating) scores – such as fatigue and appearance. In other words, while the former tended to be more obvious, the latter tended to be hidden and therefore overlooked, at least by nurses but also on occasion by patients, at interview.

So, given this variety of data, my attention focused on how it could be explained, analysed and presented.

EXPLANATIONS

Hindsight seems to have a knack of conferring upon seemingly unfathomable perplexities a clarity of explanation which belies the reality of the immediate situation. This observation must be singularly characteristic of the research process, a process where, almost inevitably, the researcher has so much invested in a project that the 'wood' of the data trends is obscured by the diversity of the 'trees' represented by individual respondents. Such is the present case. What is presented here is, it must be said, the product of some reflective rationalization process which could only take place after the event. Nevertheless, this does not negate the need to undertake such a process since, it can be argued, all resulting lessons can at least inform future projects, if not the one to hand.

The first 'rationalization' pertains to methodological rigour. My two means of data collection, as outlined above, despite the best intentions might, in fact, have diluted the strength of methodological triangulation. The SDS was clearly designed to measure the magnitude of symptoms as experienced by the patient respondents, but the interview schedule was actually eliciting more than this. While some of the topic areas of the latter did, indeed, relate to symptoms covered in the former, either explicitly (pain, appetite, etc.) or by suggestion (mobility, sickness, etc.), others were designed to identify areas where a *need* or *problem* existed (e.g. *need* for advice, aids, *problems* with finance, illness related worries, etc.). This embraces a much larger universe of content, being concerned with deficits in what might be termed a holistic integrity, rather than with a list of pathological characteristics. In other words the process may have approximated more to a theoretical triangulation (use of multiple perspectives) than the method focus (use of multiple methods) which was my intention.

But the differences between the two data collection tools extended beyond this, specifically with regard to the temporal context within which the data elicited should be viewed. The SDS particularly requested that respondents' statements should apply to the current moment in time (i.e. 'How do you feel *now?'*), while in the interview no such specifications were made. Thus my responses included the patient who rated her sleeping problem at a maximum of 5 after an isolated, particularly troublesome night yet had not thought to mention this at interview which she assumed, quite understandably, to be concerned with enduring problems encountered through the illness history. The lesson here, I now feel, is to think through clearly and then target not only the content which any tool aims to capture but also the purpose in terms of its retrospective, current or predictive relevance.

A second 'explanatory' issue is that of bias and the possibility that I might have been swaying my respondents to answer in a certain way by both the nature of the data collection instruments and by the order in which I administered them. My suspicion is that by offering a checklist of potentially relevant items, patients may have been cued to respond affirmatively simply because their mention had brought them to attention. This does not necessarily contraindicate the approach in itself, for respondents may merely have forgotten certain experiences when posed an open question on the spur of the moment. After all, researchers must accept that subjective experiences are real to a person if expressed as such – indeed, the classic example of pain is often defined in this way.

The worrying issue is not so much how important a problem is if it has not been volunteered, but the ethical one of whether the researcher has the right to bring to light (and therefore emphasize) problems which the patient has until then not been concerned about or even conscious of. This would, of course, depend upon the individual but I couldn't help noticing that certain respondents more readily picked out as stressful a greater number of items on the SDS than they had isolated at interview.

This leads to the third and related issue of subjectivity. The numbers on a scale, and even the statements at either extreme of a symptom's intensity, may mean different things to different individuals. This is, of course, why so much time and effort is given to testing such tools for reliability and validity. But there are two points which need to be highlighted here. The first is that, within a rating scale, many respondents tend not to associate with extreme descriptors (Polit and Hungler, 1987) and that this response set distorts the results.

This can be supported in my study where, for instance, only one person scored a maximum 5 for pain, within a pathological area (all patients had cancer) where one might have expected pain level to be greater than for other disease processes.

Secondly, reliability in relation to a tool looking at subjective concerns is extremely difficult to establish between respondents, but is more likely to occur over an individual's response to several items. So, what I should have been looking for, perhaps, was not how the pattern of symptom distress varied uniformly between individuals in the two data measurements but whether, within an individual's responses, the degree of correlation between the two forms was uniform over different items. In other words, given a *consistent* mismatch between the extent of, say, pain, appetite and bowel problems within one individual's responses, one should perhaps be less concerned than if no consistency became apparent.

Subjectivity in rating is but one step away from what I consider to be the main issue at stake in my particular quantitative–qualitative dilemma and that is the reliability and validity of the very concepts being studied as presented in my project. On the face of it the central issue would appear to be one of reliability – is there consistency in the meaning attached to a symptom/ need between the researcher and the respondent? If there is, then even if validity cannot be upheld, the fact that there is a shared interpretation of the subjects being discussed means that responses are surely useful and have meaning. (Though even this cannot, of course, be assumed, as Williams *et al.* (1991) so intriguingly point out in an exercise consisting of a retrospective reclassification by respondents into groups they had previously been assigned to by the researchers.)

My problem, however, was not so much researcher–respondent differences (though this may have been influential, given the nurse- as opposed to patient-derived categories in the interview schedule) but differences *within* a respondent's answers *vis à vis* the two different schedules. And this, to me, suggests a question of (construct) validity; am I measuring the same, specific thing when I suggest a number of particular symptoms as when I ask an open question regarding potential problem areas?

I see two ways of looking at this issue, the first based on a semantic approach, the second more methodological in nature.

Firstly, it is obvious in comparing my two tools that, while some items are directly reproduced (pain, appetite, bowels) and others are unique to one or the other (mood, concentration on the SDS, aids, advice in the interview), there are a few items which are, to all intents and purposes, equivalent. For instance, nausea equates easily with sickness, insomnia with sleep problems and fatigue with tiredness. At least it does from the research end, but then researchers are always on the lookout for ways of pigeon-holing and categorizing! From the layman's perspective, the words might conjure up very different images or even hold no meaning at all.

I was very conscious of this as I talked to individuals ranging from the highly articulate and forthcoming to the quiet type one needed to 'probe'. When (as happened) a patient mentioned anxiety at interview but had not ticked mood change on the SDS, or admitted to forgetfulness but omitted memory problems – and these in addition to the obvious examples quoted above – would they, given a different perspective, have included the SDS items as expressing the same concepts in different ways? If so, would one be entitled, when it came to data analysis, to classify them under these prearranged terms? Conversely, respondents themselves may have unconsciously gone through the 'reclassification' process themselves and approximated their responses to categories nearest to those representing their perceptual experience. If this 'slotting in' was not undertaken, one wonders how many issues may simply have been neglected altogether.

In this semantic approach, then, wording can be seen as paramount and the moral is surely to pilot all instruments fully and, if necessary, build in facilities for clarification of any concept, perhaps using alternative phrases.

The second angle from which to address validity is methodological. In essence, this comes back to the whole quantitative–qualitative issue which was also at the centre of the study by Williams *et al.* (1991), cited above. These authors, in concluding that 'it should not be unexpected that there will be discrepancies between what the statistical analysis provides and the subjective response of the interviewed (nurse)' (p. 918), challenge the assumption made in traditional research approaches that it actually matters if lines of enquiry do not converge.

The point is that the researcher is looking for different types of 'evidence'. Quantitative data are reductionist, prestripped for the purpose of comparison and generalization and concerned with manifestations rather than meanings. Qualitative data are contextual, embedded in personalized trappings and very much at the mercy of the researcher when it comes to interpretation. Williams *et al.* suggest that these discrepancies, because they focus on different levels of meaning, may provide a useful resource. So, given this, how could I 'use' my divergent findings constructively?

DATA ANALYSIS

My overall approach to data analysis was dictated by Yin's (1989) case study methodology, which advocates a synthesis of findings from the individual cases through a replication logic. This is a way of overcoming the eternal problem of external validity in studies with small samples, since generalization is to theoretical propositions rather than to populations. In practice this meant, for me, 'matching' the conclusions from each case I analysed with the findings from both the literature and the remaining cases.

However, this still begged the question of analytical methodology within each case. Yin is not prescriptive here, emphasizing that the case study approach does not limit the researcher to any one overall paradigm. My solution – some may say compromise – was to present data both quantitatively and qualitatively (though separately) and to discuss any inconsistencies within the text.

The way I did this, though, was not simplistic. My feelings were that both quantitative and qualitative data were useful, the former because, in order to match patterns, data needed to be manageable and therefore 'stripped' to a certain degree, the latter because the whole case study ethos is about tapping, in depth, the universe of processes and meanings surrounding the unit of analysis. But my view regarding the value of the two instruments was not that they were of exactly equal worth and the drawbacks to scales enumerated above (limited responses, the need to establish validity, the central tendency) plus my own experience in using them (particularly the use of set words with particular client groups) tipped the balance in favour of a greater use of the interview data.

Data presentation, therefore, consisted in a certain amount of data from the interview schedule being presented in a 'stripped' tabular form which facilitated comparison between the three respondent groups and across the nine cases. This fitted in quite easily with the 'Standard' format of my interview which was asking, in essence, whether structure and outcome criteria were met and which problem/need areas were identified and addressed by the different groups. In addition to this, a feel for how the patients experienced those things most important to them was presented through transcribed interview extracts, alongside comparative nurse based comments, where appropriate. The SDS data, though not integrated here, were not lost entirely, being incorporated in ways consistent with the Scale's validated use such as, as a correlate with numbers of visits by the nurses.

CONCLUSIONS

The rather cynical view which I expressed about the research experience at the start of this chapter is, perhaps, not diminished in the recounting. But I'm equally sure that researchers are a resilient breed and can, as Williams *et al.* (1991) advise, use apparently contradictory findings resourcefully.

In my small study looking at, among other things, the experience of terminal illness and how patients viewed their care, I chose a methodology built on the assumption that different lines of enquiry would converge around a unified picture of each individual's experience. But human beings are often too dynamic to be constrained within the limits of rigid research methods. The solution, I would suggest, to the student caught on the horns of such a paradox is to use data flexibly and imaginatively, but always with a predefined statement of the purpose of the operation. In my case, for instance, the fact that I captured the 'one-off' occurrence of a symptom alongside the more enduring experiences, by different means, said something valuable in itself about the fluctuating nature of the nursing needs which were the focus of my study – this irrespective of whether or not I could accommodate the positive versus negative assertions of that need's presence according to which tool was being administered.

I have to say that my conclusions were not too disheartening for the nursing profession. Patient based data, when compared to those from nurse based interviews, revealed a relatively small degree of mismatch in identifying problems and taking action to alleviate them, both in the quantitative tabulation and in the themes depicted in the transcribed quotations. To this extent, method triangulation did actually seem to work according to the textbook, even in an area where I least expected it to. But I would caution against the approach being seen as an answer to the researcher's prayer, nor one to be adopted lightly without thinking through the possible implications. To slightly adapt a Shakespearian truism, 'the case of true research never did run smooth!'

REFERENCES

Bell, C. and Roberts, H. (1984) *Social Researching*, Routledge and Kegan Paul, London.

Bryman, A. (1988) *Quality and Quantity in Social Research*, Contemporary Social Research 18, Unwin Hyman, London.

Denzin, N.K. (1978) *The Research Act*, 2nd edn, McGraw Hill, New York.

French, K. (1981) Methodological considerations in hospital patient opinion surveys. *International Journal of Nursing Studies*, **88**, 7–32.

McCorkle, R. and Young, K. (1978) Development of a symptom distress scale. *Cancer Nursing*, **1**, 373–8.

Polit, D.F. and Hungler, B.P. (1987) *Nursing Research: Principles and Methods*, 3rd edn, Lippincott, Philadelphia.

Spitzer, W.O., Dobson, A.J., Hall, J. *et al.* (1981) Measuring the quality of life of cancer patients. *Journal of Chronic Diseases*, **34**, 585–98.

Williams, C., Soothill, K., and Barry, J. (1991) Nursing: just a job? Do statistics tell us what we think? *Journal of Advanced Nursing*, **16**, 910–19.

Yin, R.K. (1989) *Case Study Research: Designs and Methods*, Applied Social Research Methods series Vol. 5, Sage Publications, Newbury Park, California.

9

Making sense of qualitative data

Kath Ross

INTRODUCTION AND BACKGROUND TO THE STUDY

My experience of dealing with qualitative data emerged because of a longstanding interest in the reasons why some clinical practitioners decide to change their professional orientation and become nurse educationalists.

The first opportunity to investigate this question arose in 1988/89 when, as a student on a part time 52 week research course, I was expected to carry out a small scale investigation as part of the coursework. During the discussions on what research methodology might be appropriate to investigate the question, I became fascinated by the interpretive and qualitative research approaches, especially that of 'grounded theory' (Glaser and Strauss, 1967). This fascination, compounded by the paucity of research in the topic area, permitted a legitimate attempt at a qualitative design (Field and Morse, 1985). A grounded theory methodology utilizing unstructured formal interviews (Swanson, 1986) was adopted as the data collection method.

This initial small scale investigation (Ross, 1989) enabled me both to experiment and to experience the research process. This fuelled an evolving interest in research and particularly in the complexities of qualitative research. The data from this small scale study served to highlight the need for further exploration in the topic area, as well as highlighting some of the problems of analysing qualitative data.

With this experience clearly in the forefront of my mind the

investigation was continued and extended in 1990 as part fulfilment of an MA in Sociological Research in Health Care (Ross,
1990). The 1989 investigation served as a pilot study sensitizing
me to what might be expected in a slightly larger and more
rigorous study. The analysis process within the 1989 work,
although time consuming, was achieved with relative ease when
compared with what was to follow in the 1990 study, the
subject of discussion here. In retrospect, the obvious reason for
this was that I had adopted, as the framework for analysing
the 1989 study, a relatively narrow management theory perspective. This is not to suggest that the work undertaken was
valueless; rather what is acknowledged are the limitations
of any such work where the wider dimensions of any other
relevant perspectives are not fully utilized and the data is
analysed and interpreted from a limited perspective.

It was from this experience and a widening knowledge base
in the social sciences arena that the real complexities of analysing qualitative data emerged.

ANALYSING QUALITATIVE DATA USING
GROUNDED THEORY

The method used for analysing the data in the 1990 study
followed the process of 'constant comparative analysis' (Glaser
and Strauss, 1967). This method of data collection and analysis
is concurrent so that codes, categories and themes can evolve
and be developed as they are compared with incoming data.
To facilitate this process of concurrent data collection and data
analysis, 18 interviews were conducted at 3-weekly intervals
in four clusters of between 2–5 participants in each cluster.
In 'pure' constant comparative analysis the process continues
until it is evident that further incoming data fail to raise new
codes and categories. At this point it may be suggested that
each category or theme is saturated.

This inductive approach to theory generation is highly desirable as the emerging theory is thus truly generated from the
data (Stern, 1980). However problems arise if, as is usually the
case, the research has a time period by which it must be
completed. In this instance this was a course submission deadline. This then creates a situation where the researcher is not
fully certain that the categories and themes *are* saturated and

would not continue to develop further by disclosure of new or divergent data. This can leave the researcher, in a study of this size, somewhat frustrated as she cannot be sure at this point that an interpretation is realistic or appropriate since the analysis process may be considered as incomplete.

In the majority of texts the process of qualitative analysis is described in a linear and systematic way, with the end result, the report, neatly describing the phenomena under investigation. This portrayal is far more schematic than the actual experience. In this study the only linear aspect was that of a reasonably sane and rational individual gradually disappearing deeper and deeper into the mass of data as the efforts of coding and categorizing progressed! However, although the experience was uncomfortable, all-consuming and sometimes frustrating, the feeling of being able to leave the process through arriving at an understanding of the area and en route perhaps demonstrating one's creative ability made the whole experience very rewarding, fulfilling and worthwhile. It is this very experience that I endeavour to capture here.

THE ANALYSIS PROCESS

The analysis process lasted the span of the 18 interviews, ten weeks in total. After the first five interviews the task of analysis was seen as straightforward. The framework described in the literature by Maxwell and Maxwell (1980), which had been used and adapted in the light of the 1989 study, gave a logical and systematic approach to be followed, i.e.:

1. Collection of empirical data;
2. Concept formation:
   — code the data
   — cluster the codes into initial small categories;
3. Concept and theme development:
   — collapse these small categories into larger categories;
4. Concept modification and theme integration:
   — encapsulate these large categories into themes which explain the phenomena.

It is true to say that this framework for analysis was adhered to throughout the study although, as previously mentioned, in the real situation phases were far from linear as I oscillated

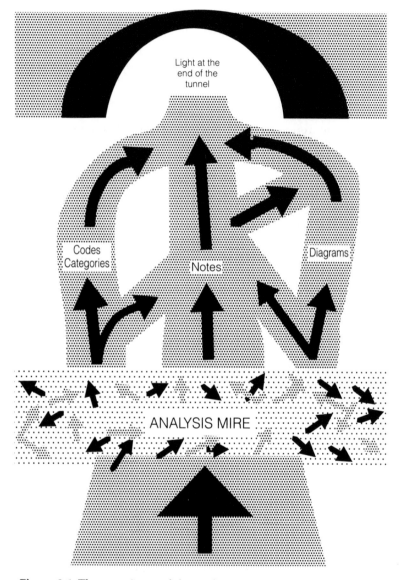

Figure 9.1 The experience of the analysis process.

backwards and forwards between the phases to ensure that the process was as valid and reliable as possible.

Figure 9.1 represents the actual experience that I feel I went through and it is with the aid of this diagram that some of the complexities of the analysis process may be viewed, along with the ways of achieving an acceptable level of clarity and interpretation.

THE ANALYSIS MIRE

The approach to what I call 'the analysis mire' was relatively straightforward, albeit time consuming. Each interview was transcribed as soon as possible after the event and in most cases this occurred after each cluster of allotted interviews. This transcription, which I undertook personally despite the lack of adequate typing skills, proved invaluable as it not only facilitated a second chance to listen to the data but more importantly it allowed me to contextualize the data by listening to the intonations and emphasis used by the participants. This highlighted the value of recording the conversations, as the spontaneous feelings of what had been said directly after the interview were superseded or enhanced by other factors clearly volunteered and heard on the interview tapes.

Although this initial process was crucial for getting me em-erged in the data it was far more time consuming than originally estimated, something which Burgess (1984) confirms is usually the case. Most interviews lasted 50 minutes, took an average of five hours to type up and yielded approximately 16 transcript pages. Each page had an extended margin on the right hand side to enable codes to be added.

Additional to this exercise, a brief written resumé relating to my experience of each interview had been documented. At the time I started to do this I was not sure of its value. However it became an interesting and important issue related to the reliability of the research method. Within the brief example quoted below, it can be seen that the quality of the interview may have been affected by the circumstances in which the interview took place. (For the interview to which this example pertained, the transcription was examined very closely to en-sure that the same level and variety of questioning and probing had occurred, since my performance could well have been impeded by the circumstances as described.)

This was a very strange experience as this interview was conducted at a large table in the middle of a Nightingale type ward. The participant, with the exception of one very inexperienced seconded student, was the only carer in sight. This did not seem to bother the participant but I was very bemused as I could see the need for her skills required in the ward whilst the interview was in progress. We were also interrupted once by a telephone and then by a half hour social 'chit chat' with a teacher who appeared on the ward that I had met in a previous post. However it was a very relaxed interview.

CONCEPT AND THEME FORMATION AND DEVELOPMENT

The following extracts from one interview demonstrate how 'coding' was approached. They do not reflect the whole content of the interview and issues pertinent to the research question but do raise a number of pertinent areas. Relevant data has been **highlighted** in the text with the coding alongside.

TRANSCRIPTION   CODE

K When did you start thinking that you might be a teacher?

P I have always been quite interested in teaching, **I think really it was while I was** *Timing of decision* **doing the ITU course I was enjoying studying again.** I think there are several reasons, this will sound dreadful. **You watch people** *Professional reason* **doing things and you realize that perhaps** *for wanting to* **they are not doing them the right way and** *educate* **they do not understand why they are doing them.** For example whilst I was doing the ITU course, when I asked why people were doing things they would say, 'that is how we do it here' and you could not actually get a proper answer. That was the answer I was getting back frequently.

TRANSCRIPTION	CODE

I think that nurses need to be taught pro-perly and if they are taught properly they can think a bit more for themselves. It sounds as if I am going to change the world. There is no way that I can do that sing-lehanded but I just feel that if they are taught the right thing then they can become more thinking than doing.

Professional reason for wanting to educate

(The interview continued with the participant de-scribing, with enthusiasm, her present role, in-cluding the positive responses she had from any teaching she embarked upon.)

K You are obviously doing well clinically. Have you considered continuing in a type of clinical role?

P **I don't want to go further into clinical management. The nurse management struc-ture has changed so many times in the 11 years I have been nursing and it is a very uncertain area of nursing to get into.** The only step I can go from here is a senior sister's post and they come up fairly rarely, so really there isn't anywhere for me to go **apart from doing something like transplant coordination or infection control and that does not really interest me.**

Exclusion of management as a career move

Exclusion of specialist nurse role as a career move

K If you could have one of these senior sister's posts, is that where you would choose to be?

P Perhaps for a short while but even from there **I would still like to go into teaching because of financial reasons. In education the financial rewards in several years' time are quite attractive.** The other thing about clinical work, even as a sister **I am still doing half my shifts a month on night duty, which**

Financial reason for teaching

Night duty disliked in present role

TRANSCRIPTION	CODE
I actually find very difficult. It wasn't too bad when I was younger. **Seven long nights a month make me feel really tired and socially it isn't good. So from the social and the financial thing with the mortgage and things.** They perhaps shouldn't matter but they do, you know. For that in itself education is quite attractive.	*Social implications of night duty, undesirable in present role*

From these extracts it can be seen that coding the data was carried out by taking each interview, line by line, and highlighting data raised by the participant which had relevance for the research question. On the right hand side of the page a word or words, explaining what was being said, summarized or typified the verbatim data. This coding system generated 62 codes from the first five interviews. After a further five interviews this was increased to 89.

A number of research issues became evident at this point and needed consideration before the research and analysis could continue. The first pertained to my interview style. I felt it essential that a second person viewed a selection of the transcripts to ensure that the chosen method, unstructured interviews, was in fact being used and that I was not imposing a structure by my interview technique. Secondly I also wanted to verify that the data was relevant to the research question.

Thirdly I wanted to ensure that the verbatim data segments highlighted were appropriate and that a degree of researcher bias had not been introduced by interpreting rather than representing, or highlighting only data which fulfilled any preconceived ideas of my own. To facilitate this, after the first ten interviews a fellow student examined two randomly selected transcribed interviews where the codes and any notes had been removed. There was confirmation that the data method used was relevant and consistent, including the relevance of the areas that had been probed to give rich qualitative data.

It was an immense relief to receive feedback indicating that the participants had been facilitated in 'telling their own story'; however, the second issue of highlighting and coding the data raised concern. Although the verbatim data highlighted was consistent with the fellow student's, coding was, in some cases, sufficiently different as to suggest that some of the codes were interpretive rather than representative. Therefore a review of the interviews to date took place in order to adjust the codes appropriately.

ENTERING THE MIRE

Once a number of codes had been adjusted the verbatim data was amalgamated under the code headings. The use of the cutting and pasting facility on the wordprocessor was invaluable here! It was a long and laborious task to ensure that all the highlighted verbatim data from each transcribed interview was placed next to similar data from other interviews, under the appropriate code. The purpose of this exercise was twofold. Firstly it enabled each code to be viewed for internal consistency and secondly it assisted the process of category formation, by which each code could be compared with others to consider whether they could be grouped together because they gave a specific meaning or pattern. It was hoped that this would ensure that the categories arose from the data rather than being imposed by any predetermined categorization.

In theory this all sounds very straightforward, but I was totally unprepared for the amount of amalgamated data, which produced a 60-page document. This was overwhelming considering there were still eight interviews to be undertaken. It was fortunate at this point that a research support group, set up in Oxford, provided a discussion forum for me. In an hour long presentation session I was able to discuss the research to date and raise the problems I was having with the data analysis. This was an important landmark as not only were the group constructively critical of my analysis process but they also gave me positive feedback. This encouraged me and gave me the necessary impetus to continue. This hour presentation and discussion confirmed the need to break some of the codes down further, with the notion that this would give more appropriate categorization from a more rigorous approach.

'Personal considerations' was an initial code which I had used to group together several what I thought were related issues. These included, for example, working conditions such as night duty, economic reasons such as a need for higher paid work in the present economic climate and a number of areas related to working mothers. This coding example identifies several separate components of an interpretive rather than a representative code. It clearly demonstrates that these are very different pieces of data which together do have some meaning but taken separately can start to account for much wider socio-economic, structural situations which might have impinged on the decision making process to move from clinical work into education.

Going back to the data created a further opportunity to recall the data and become saturated by being fully engaged in understanding what the data were saying. Within this task it became obvious that I must write down what I thought the data were saying. A number of notes (as seen in Figure 9.1) were generated and the following one is typical of tentative thoughts.

The teaching aspect of their clinical role they seem to enjoy, as they did with the clinical nursing (majority). When viewing clinical nursing they seem to consider career development in either their clinical role or management. However they cannot develop their clinical career without management or without unsocial hours. Development in management was seen by most as undesirable. The clinical specialist role, if mentioned, either included unsocial hours or was not part of the structure in their area of expertise.

It also seems to be the case that the educational option is seen by a number of participants as reducing job conflict, enabling autonomy, maintaining clinical input and excludes areas of jobs that these participants find dissatisfying. The educational environment is also seen as friendly and therefore supportive and the staff enthusiastic.

Notes such as these were considered incomplete as it could have been the case that they only represented the data that I wished to hear. This did nothing to lift the increasing discomfort as I continued my pathway deeper into the mire. I was at a loss as to which way to go next. No matter how much the codes were reformed together they failed to produce meaningful categories where the relationship between them could be identified.

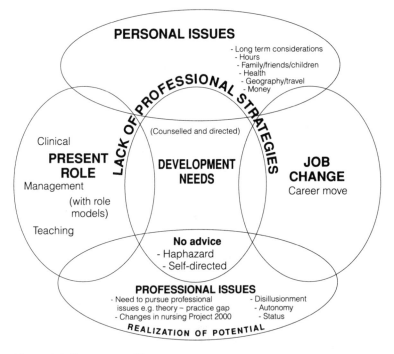

Figure 9.2 Present world.

In desperation I started drawing rough diagrams which conceptually represented what the data seemed to be saying. At first this was done in an uncommitted way, feeling that the diagram might materialize into a very neat plausible explanation which might not, however, really represent the data but suited any conscious or subconscious preconceived views. The first rough diagram (Figure 9.2) attempted to conceptualize the scope of the data and the many factors that affected the individual's decision making process. This clearly demonstrated that categories were not mutually exclusive but overlapped and affected each other. It became clear that if the notes and a thorough revisit of the codes and initial categories occurred, that this diagramming, if developed, had the potential to produce the required understanding.

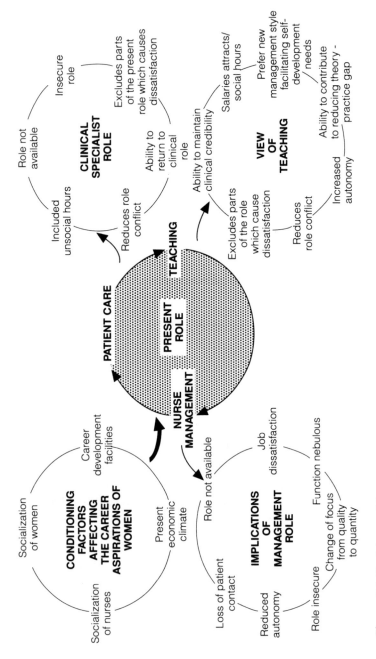

Figure 9.3 Decision making process.

ESCAPING THE MIRE

The above solution produced the breakthrough. There was suddenly a feeling of enlightenment as at last the totality of the data was beginning to make sense and the drawings demonstrated some form of data integration, giving an albeit preliminary picture of the decision making process. It was through this initial diagram, integrated with the codes, categories, notes and incoming data from the last eight interviews, that the more complex diagram (Figure 9.3) evolved. This illuminated the highly complex and multidimensional nature of the topic which clearly encompassed so much more than I thought was the case in my earlier 1989 investigation.

EMERGENCE OF THE THEORETICAL PERSPECTIVE

Throughout my time in the mire I was constantly conscious of the need to analyse the data at two levels. Firstly there was the basic level where the totality of the data could be understood and a descriptive account could be given. Secondly, at a higher level of interpretation, the data could be explained and supported in the context of the social world.

Achieving this second level proved as tortuous a pathway as gaining a good understanding at the basic level of data analysis. In order to achieve this higher level of understanding a sociological perspective was sought and was provided by Giddens' (1979) concept of 'agency and structure'. This provided the framework by which the data related to areas outside the control of nursing, for example economics, could be examined. This increased the speed of analysis and facilitated a wider understanding of the phenomena. This interpretive level of the analysis process proved an exciting aspect as not only did it give this rich data more meaning but it also enabled a channel to increase its external validity by comparing the data with other works, both inside and outside nursing.

It would have been so easy at this stage to stop improving the rigour of the analysis process and concentrate on the final interpretation, that which synthesized the literature with the levels of analysis. However it seemed that one very important phase to date had been omitted, that of checking the internal validity of the data with the participants to ensure that the

basic level of analysis represented the reality of these participants' decision making processes.

To this end and with the deadline for submission four weeks
away, a written account of the basic level of analysis, describing the concepts and themes as identified in Figure 9.3,
was sent to the participants in an amalgamated form. Each
participant was requested to read the document as quickly as
possible with the purpose of being constructively critical, specifically highlighting areas where the descriptions did not depict
their reality or omissions were evident. Fifty-six percent of the
participants responded and nine out of ten of these participants responded positively to the account. Three out of the
ten acknowledged the reality of some of the data which other
participants had offered which they themselves had not raised
in their interviews. One participant commented that insuf-
ficient emphasis had been placed on the views of the minority
in one section.

This enabled a review of the data and a change in the subsequent and final submitted written account. It is acknowledged that the response rate was low. This may not have been
the case if the expected time to receive, read, comment and
return the document had been greater than seven days. Com-
pounding this situation was the length of the account, 15 pages,
which must have been offputting to even the most willing
participants! I was deeply indebted to those who were able to
reply as even this low response gave positive encouragement
and fuelled progress in the last phase of full integration of both
the basic and interpretive analysis levels.

As with all the activities that have been described so far
these did not occur in isolation from one another. Whilst writing and awaiting the participants' replies to the descriptive account, an intense revisiting of the original literature
reviewed, with extension into new literature, occurred.
The literature from an original review was compared with
the analysed data ready for assimilation into the final report.
Simultaneously a new range of literature, which had been
highlighted through data analysis and the theoretical perspective of 'agency and structure', was also being considered.

This final phase prior to writing the report seemed absolutely
essential. It was also obvious, given the variety of literature
directions, that the data indicated the potentially impossible

task of exploring all the relevant literature, given the advancing submission deadline. Due to this situation it was decided that the literature should be constrained to the main themes and concepts that had emerged from the analysis process. Therefore a 'dip' into the literature relating to socialization of women and nurses, role conflict and strain, bureaucratic organizations, women and work and the division of labour in the health service followed. This illuminated further the complexities of the topic under study and raised the very different perspectives through which the interpretation could take place. It was only through the theoretical perspective and the data supported by the literature that the complexity of the topic could be represented in an organized manner for the reader to understand.

One week prior to the submission deadline a full draft of the analysis chapter was finished. The enormous relief at completing a task which had seemed impossible six weeks earlier cannot be overestimated. It had been such a tiring all-consuming process. The interviewing, transcribing, coding, note making, diagramming and thinking had not only taken over my personal life but also the mass of paper generated had taken over any spare floor space in the family home! Reassembling the rooms and carrying out 'neglected' household chores now proved a delight!!

This delight I felt was, however, diminished by the dissatisfaction of an incomplete study which, given more time and energy, would hopefully have produced categories that were saturated, thus giving the tentative interpretation more strength or differing emphasis. It was only some months after the completion of the dissertation that the real value of carrying out such a process was realized, not only for the personal achievement in creative terms but for the very small contribution that the study has made to my understanding of nursing, women and women's work.

WHAT ABOUT QUANTIFYING THE QUALITATIVE DATA?

It is clear from the methods of analysis described that a decision to exclude any level of quantitative analysis occurred. It was a difficult decision which was re-evaluated at various points in the analysis process. Eventually the ambivalence in this area was resolved because I felt that representation in a numerical way would detract from the richness of the data given to me by the participants. The opportunity to extract the real numerical value by further interviewing, using a more focused approach, was also not a realistic option because of time constraints. It is perhaps worth stating that given the nature of the topic and the qualitative research methodology utilized, the use of quantitative analysis in an area such as this remains highly debatable (Stern, 1991).

What remains clear to me is that embarking on qualitative analysis is truly a creative, dynamic and rigorous process for those willing to engage themselves in such a convoluted adventure.

Acknowledgement

I would like to thank Anthony Knipe, AVA technician in the Department of Health Care Studies, Oxford Polytechnic, Oxford, for all his work on the diagrams.

REFERENCES

Burgess, R. (1984) *In the Field – An Introduction to Field Research*, George Allen and Unwin, Boston.

Field P.A. and Morse, J.M. (1985) *Nursing Research – The Application of Qualitative Approaches*, Croom Helm, London, Chapter 1.

Giddens, A. (1979) *Central Problems in Social Theory: Action, Structure and Contradictions in Social Analysis*, Macmillan Press Ltd, London.

Glaser, B. and Strauss, A. (1967) *The Discovery of Grounded Theory: Strategies for Qualitative Research*, Weidenfeld and Nicolson, London.

Maxwell, E. and Maxwell, R. (1980) Cited in Stern, P., Grounded theory methodology: its uses and processes. *Image*, 12(1), 20–3.

Ross, K. (1989) *Why Clinical Practitioners Decide to Become Educationalists.* Paper presented at Research in Clinical Nursing Conference, John Radcliffe Academic Centre, Oxford, May 16.

Ross, K. (1990) Nurse education – a personal and professional choice. Warwick University. M.A. Dissertation.

Stern, P.N. (1980) Grounded theory methodology: its uses and process. *Image*, 12(1), 20–3.

Stern, P.N. (1991) Are counting and coding a capella appropriate in qualitative research? in *Qualitative Nursing Research: A Contemporary Dialogue*, (ed. J.M. Morse), Sage Publications, London.

Swanson, W. (1986) The formal qualitative interview, in *From Practice to Grounded Theory: Qualitative Research in Nursing*, (eds J. Chenitz and W. Swanson), Addison-Wesley, California, Chapter 6.

10

Leaping to the right conclusions? The problems of confounding and measurement in a ward based nursing research project

Sophie Hyndman

INTRODUCTION

In the most intelligent races, as among the Parisians, there are a large number of women whose brains are closer in size to those of gorillas than to the most developed male brains. This inferiority is so obvious that no one can contest it for a moment; only its degree is worth discussion. All psychologists who have studied the intelligence of women, as well as poets and novelists, recognize today that they represent the most inferior forms of human evolution and that they are closer to children and savages than to an adult, civilized man. They excel in fickleness, inconstancy, absence of thought and logic, and incapacity to reason. Without doubt there exist some distinguished women, very superior to the average man, but they are as exceptional as the birth of any monstrosity, as, for example, of a gorilla with two heads; consequently, we may neglect them entirely.

(Gustave Le Bon, 1879, pp. 60–61)

In his book *The Mismeasure of Man*, Stephen Jay Gould (1981) relates the incredible history of nineteenth century craniometry. Le Bon, quoted above in his discussion of data generated by

Paul Broca, believed that size of brain was related to intelligence. On the basis of numerous investigations, they concluded that because women had smaller brains than men, they were less intelligent. Although aware that factors such as body size affected brain size, they chose to ignore these measures. Gould reworked the original data taking into account height and age and proposed a number of other factors which are now known to influence brain size. We can be comforted that he concludes, 'Broca's data do not permit any confident claim that men have bigger brains than women'.

One might reasonably ask what all this has to do with nursing research. In fact the above study illustrates one of the problems common to many research projects and one which we had to face in our study: the problem of confounding and the measurement of outcome.

In the study described above, the variables of sex and brain size were related to other factors, for example, height and age. Factors which are wholly or partially related to a variable of interest in a study but are not of direct interest are known as confounding factors. If you are unaware of these factors or take no steps to control them, you can easily leap to the wrong conclusions (and what conclusions!).

THE ODySSSy PROJECT

The Royal College of Nursing ODySSSy Project was set up in 1989 with a three year grant from the Department of Health. The project aimed to evaluate a quality assurance package for nurses, the Dynamic Standard Setting System (RCN Standards of Care, 1990).

The Dynamic Standard Setting System (DySSSy) involves a group of nurses on a ward working with a trained facilitator to improve an area of care. To do this, they identify criteria which cover everything they need, everything they need to do and everything they hope to achieve in terms of patients' care. These criteria are built into a standard form which the nurses then use to evaluate their current practice and to improve it, where criteria they have identified have not been met.

DySSSy was beginning to spread around health authorities and even abroad and its popularity prompted the question:

'Does it really work?'. One of the ODySSSy Project's objectives, therefore, was to see whether nurses setting a standard
on post-operative pain management in a surgical setting using
the system could have an effect on the way patients recovered
and the way they experienced care. The ODySSSy Project
was basically trying to link the process of setting standards to
patient outcome.

The nature of DySSSy itself made relating process to outcome rather difficult. Ideally one would like to perform an
experiment where a group of wards would set standards and
a group of wards would act as controls. Wards would be
randomly assigned to the experimental condition and grouped
in an analysis at the end of the study data collection. We had
two things to consider in approaching our design. The first
question related to how amenable DySSSy really was to a
true experimental design as the process of DySSSy is highly
individual to the standard setting group and the ward undertaking it. The possibility of change in patient outcome would
be highly dependent on the groups themselves and the topic of
post-operative pain management might be interpreted in many
ways, from preoperative information giving to complementary
therapy. How well the group functioned together would be
of paramount importance in determining the pace and the
ultimate success or failure of the process. Even if changes were
seen, the chances that they would be seen at the same time on
each ward were very small. This would make it unwise to
lump all the wards together in one analysis – the progress
of one ward might well be hidden by the failure of another.
You would, in effect, be combining the results of different
interventions.

A second question related to the large amount of variation
that would exist in the sample of wards. It would be very
difficult to detect the effects of DySSSy on patient outcome
through the mist of the variation in outcomes that would already exist between the wards in the experiment. To do this
successfully, we would require a very large number of wards
and this was not within our financial reach! For these reasons,
it was decided that we would have to approach the evaluation
of DySSSy using a quasi-experimental design in which we
would have ten wards, paired within five hospitals. One in
each pair would implement DySSSy, the other would act as a

'quasi' control. We would look at changes over 14 months in patient outcome in the two wards.

CONFOUNDING IN THE RELATION OF PROCESS TO OUTCOME

Doris Bloch wrote in a paper in 1980, 'When it comes to process–outcome assessment, do not send a boy to do a man's job' and she was not joking. When you take an aspirin for a headache, the pain goes away and it seems obvious that it goes away because an aspirin was taken. Unfortunately, in a health care setting at least, relating process to outcome is not as simple as it seems. As Williamson stated in 1971, 'The evaluation of patient care requires the consideration of hundreds of variables'.

The process of care is everything that practitioners *do* when caring for a patient. It is the action taken in order to achieve specified patient outcomes. In terms of an evaluation research project, the process may be the nursing intervention under investigation, a new method of teaching patients, a new method of lifting patients, a new analgesia, etc.

Patient outcomes are what happens to the patient as a result of the care given. In a research project, they are usually defined in relation to the intervention under scrutiny, the predicted outcome resulting from the intervention. As process can be almost any intervention, so outcomes can cover a whole range of areas, including the various stages and dimensions of recovery (Starfield, 1974). Satisfaction is also a measure of how a patient has experienced the health care they have received and the satisfaction of the patient can therefore be seen as an outcome of the care process in its broadest sense.

What were the processes and outcomes in the ODySSSy Project and why should confounding pose such a problem? The process under investigation was standard setting. The expected outcomes might firstly relate to the area on which the standard was set, post-operative pain management. Secondly it was hoped that by generally raising awareness of care issues, there might be some broader, more general effect on patients. In theory it all sounds straightforward, but in practice?

If the process is standard setting, we had to think of what 'standard setting' really meant; it meant the process of training facilitators, of facilitators working successfully with staff, staff taking on board the idea of standard setting, managing to find the time to set standards, setting standards well, using their standard to describe, audit and evaluate their care.

In finding outcomes to measure we looked at the pain experienced by patients and the recovery and satisfaction of patients. These are affected by more than just the nursing process. They are affected firstly by the patients themselves: their condition, their expectations, their background. Outcomes are affected by the nursing staff: how many there are, the skill mix, their personalities, how well they communicate with each other, their competence. They are affected by the surgeon and the other members of the health care team: their competence, their personalities, how they get on together. They are affected by the ward environment: how comfortable the beds are, the decor and so on.

Confounding factors are also known as 'intervening variables'. It is easy to see why. They can intervene to confuse the variables of interest at so many points in the journey from process to outcome. ODySSSy might well have an effect on the patients, but how on earth do you go about disentangling that effect from all these other effects?

If we had been able to have a large number of wards in the study, at least some of the confounding variables associated with specific wards would have been randomly distributed between the experimental and the control groups. In the quasi-experiment, we did not have this luxury and ward differences that could influence outcome could be concentrated in either ward in the pairs being compared. To make things more complicated we had to consider the fact that these confounding variables might change during the course of the study. Even if we managed to match pairs of wards successfully at the start, there was no guarantee that they would still be matched a month later.

The following sections discuss the various factors we had to consider in the selecting of our wards and the interpreting of our data. The first part deals with confounding factors which were ward related and thus were more important to bear in mind in the quasi-experiment. The second part deals with other possible sources of confounding that we also had to consider.

WARD BASED CONFOUNDING FACTORS

The patients

A first consideration were the patients. Patients from different backgrounds may perceive their health differently before they even get to hospital. In the ODySSSy Project, it had been decided that if DySSSy would work in a busy surgical ward it would work anywhere. A great way to test the effectiveness of a tool, you might agree, but perhaps not the most amenable setting for this kind of research. Surgical wards are full of different people undergoing different operations for different complaints.

There are very well documented differences in the mortality and morbidity of different social groups (Townsend and Davidson, 1982) and other studies have shown that the reporting of subjective health amongst populations varies according to background (e.g. Bucquet and Curtis, 1986). Satisfaction with care has also been shown to vary with these patient characteristics.

What condition a patient has and how serious it is will inevitably contribute to their physical recovery. In one study, Hegyvary and Haussmann (1976a) found a surprising association between what they considered good quality nursing and the poorer physical condition of patients. The authors suspected that this was in fact due to the more seriously ill patients being nursed more carefully. If they had not considered this as a possibility, their conclusion might simply have been that good quality nursing is associated with poor patient outcomes.

Psychologists have been very interested in the role played by factors such as personality and state of mind in recovery (Mathews and Ridgeway, 1981) and much effort has been put into studying the links between preoperative anxiety in relation to post-operative stress (Boore, 1978). This has shown the importance of a patient's feelings and personality in relation to the recovery process.

In the comparison of two wards where one is undergoing an intervention, one ward may have patients who are more seriously ill than those in another ward. Different illnesses are specific to different sexes and so again, comparing wards with different sex ratios on factors such as pain and recovery may be misleading. Not many women are going to have prostate problems and not many men are going to have hysterectomies! Diseases such as cancer are associated with increased anxiety in a patient and this in turn may have an effect on recovery and well-being. If illnesses are different then patients' outcomes are going to vary regardless of the care they receive.

One would imagine that patients of all personalities and coping abilities might be represented in all wards and that there would be no reason why a particular type of person might be concentrated in one ward rather than another. However, if wards of different specialities or types were compared, for example a psychiatric ward and a surgical ward, or an NHS and a private ward, the type of patients you might get in one may be very different from those you might get in the other.

In the ODySSSy Project, to compare patient outcomes on wards without thinking about how the patients on the wards might differ could have been misleading. Wards can have patients of different sexes, ages, backgrounds and personalities. It was evident that we would have to think about the possible effects of these factors on the outcomes of interest. Pairing the wards within hospitals helped to an extent. In this way it was hoped that there were no large socioeconomic differences between patients in the two wards. It would probably have been unwise to compare one ward in the stockbroker belt with another ward in the industrial North East.

We tried very hard to select pairs of wards which were comparable in terms of patient mix. Part of the selection process involved looking at the types of operations that took place on the wards. In some ways the problems of differing operations were exacerbated by choosing wards in the same hospital. We found that wards within a surgical unit tended to specialize so that whilst one ward might be mainly concerned with general surgery, it would have a heavy bias towards urology or vascular surgery. This was potentially problematic, as operation type could well influence the pain experienced by a patient. Another point to consider is that different operations are associated with different habits and these are related to patients' background. A ward with a heavy vascular bias may have more smokers on it and smoking is related to social class. The role of patients' personality was harder to determine; however, all the wards we selected were NHS wards and as they were all surgical wards, there was no reason to suppose that one ward would be over-represented by a certain personality type.

As well as trying to select wards with patients in mind, we also collected background information on all the patients in the study which covered those characteristics that could influence the outcomes we were interested in. These included the patient's age, sex, operation type, their occupation, whether they lived alone and whether they had experienced surgery before. This enabled us to build these variables into the analysis to see how the wards being compared differed and to see how significant an effect they were having on outcomes.

Ward staff variables

The skill and abilities of individual ward staff will be important in determining aspects of patient outcome. Obviously if a surgeon cannot perform the technical aspects of care properly, the patient will suffer and recovery may well be slower. Studies such as the Confidential Enquiry into Perioperative Death (Buck *et al.*, 1987) imply there is a great deal of variation in the incidence of perioperative death and some of this might be explained by competence.

The actual number of staff, their skill mix, training, personalities and abilities of the health care team may well be ward specific and might affect patient outcome. Not all patients will get on with their carers and vice versa. This in itself can have quite an effect on the experience of care a patient has.

The level and quality of communication between the provider of care and the patient appears to influence subsequent satisfaction (McGhee, 1961) and the level of confidence in medical care can also be important (Weiss, 1988).

We had to bear in mind that these processes may be having an effect on the outcomes we were interested in. We collected information every four months from the ward sister that looked at the practical aspects of staffing such as staff:bed ratio, staff numbers, skill mix, bank and agency staff. We also tried to gauge the ward atmosphere, looking at how well the ward sister felt the nursing staff communicated with other health professionals and how long a staff nurse would usually stay on the ward. These were obviously very rough proxies for the rather intangible aspects of ward life we were trying to rate, but they were better than nothing!

Organizational characteristics

Another consideration was the potential effect that different organizations could have on both the process and the outcomes being examined. Salmon (1985), quoted in Robinson, Strong and Elkan (1989), described the National Health Service as '191 local health services rather than a national health service which operates in 191 districts'. The Health Service is far from uniform and even within one health care setting, there can be a great deal of variation in factors that might affect patient outcomes.

Organizational characteristics can affect outcome directly by influencing the patient or indirectly by providing particular resources, regimes, staff and equipment which may in turn affect outcome. Patient satisfaction, for example, may be affected by the decor of the wards, the type of bed and ward layout. Patients' recovery may be affected by the type of equipment available to the ward or they may be subject to an admissions or discharge policy. Length of stay, a commonly used indicator of recovery, may well reflect pressures or policies relating to bed allocation (Johnston, 1986); analgesia use may well be subject to availability or hospital and ward policies (Boore, 1978).

It was apparent that differences did exist between units and hospitals and this in turn might impact upon outcomes of care. Pairing the wards within hospitals avoided some of the differences that could occur in the organization between hospitals. Having said that, hospital initiatives can influence different wards at different times. As the ODySSSy Project was being set up, so too was Project 2000, resource mangement and other quality assurance activities. We collected information on all these possible confounders and wards were paired on structural criteria known to influence outcomes, for example ward layout, organization of care, satisfaction with equipment. It was not always possible to predict everything – the Gulf War caused some disruption to the hospitals involved with the ODySSSy Project.

OTHER CONFOUNDING VARIABLES

Other members of the health care team

Patient outcomes at any stage of care are the product of a number of processes. It is important to be aware of the many people who have played a part in those outcomes. For example, if the surgeons differed on one of the pair of wards being compared in the project, their different surgical techniques might easily affect the post-operative experiences of patients, even if those patients had the same operations. It is usually unrealistic to attribute general recovery solely to one member of the health care team.

In trying to isolate the impact nurses using DySSSy might have from the impact of other members of the health care team, it was important to try and break down exactly 'who is responsible for what'. To do this, we had to specify carefully the outcomes that could be largely attributed to the nurses, rather than any other group of practitioners. This was not easy. Horn (1980) points out that 'Nursing lacks empirically tested indicators that reflect the impact of nursing care'. Often the role the nurse plays in a patient's recovery is subtle and hard to define; as Hegyvary and Haussmann (1976a) suggest, 'Outcome assessment in nursing is complicated by the fact that much of nursing is directed toward psychosocial problems, an area in which there are significant measurement difficulties'.

Another problem is that the actual impact of nursing care, especially care influencing psychosocial aspects of the patient, may not be immediately apparent. Again, Hegyvary and Haussmann (1976b) point out that 'The majority of nursing outcomes may not be evident until discharge or thereafter'. It was therefore important to consider outcome after patients had been discharged. Unfortunately, it is at this stage that a host of other social and environmental factors come into play.

To measure these aspects of nursing, careful thought had to be given to outcome tools that might be used to pick up the more social and emotional aspects of recovery that might be influenced by DySSSy. We attempted to identify outcome measures that would relate to nursing care. It was not very easy. Pain management, although within the field of nursing, also has a lot to do with other disciplines. The less easily identified effects of DySSSy on the 'awareness' of nurses was very difficult to measure in terms of nursing related outcomes. In the end, we used some fairly general measures that we hoped would reflect the more nursing oriented dimensions of patient outcome. These included looking at anxiety and depression, aspects of recovery over which the nurse might be expected to exert some control, and pain.

Measurement

It is not at all unusual to find that, within a sample, variable measurement error accounts for 20–30% of the variance of measures.

(Pollard, Bobbit and Bergner, 1978)

If measures are appropriate, sensitive and specific they are far less likely to avoid picking up variation due to confounding factors. Much of the discussion surrounding the selection and development of measurement tools and many of the quality assurance systems which involve the use of such tools stress the importance of using or developing *valid* and *reliable* measures. A valid measure is one that actually measures what you set out to measure. There are a number of different forms of validity (for example, content, criterion and construct validity) and these are discussed elsewhere in detail (Horn, 1980). A reliable measure is one that measures what you want it to measure *accurately* and *consistently*. For example, if the same measure were to be used on the same patient in the same circumstances but, for example, at a different time, it should produce the same results. A measure used on the same subject at the same time but by different people should also yield the same results (inter-rater reliability). A valid measure is not necessarily reliable. For example, a pain scale is valid because it measures pain, but it is not always reliable, as pain is subjective and will vary considerably according to a large number of factors. Similarly, a reliable measure is not always valid; you can consistently measure the wrong thing!

When we were trying to choose measures for the project, we had to look for those which were valid and reliable. It helped to ask whether the measure being used was firstly appropriate to the setting where we wanted to use it secondly, whether it was sensitive to the aspect of care we were trying to measure and thirdly, whether it was specific to the thing we were measuring.

Data sources

For reliable measurement, we had to think about the data sources being used. For example, a commonly used source of data are the nursing and medical records. An important thing to consider here is how valid and reliable is this documentation? Boore (1978) wanted to look at the incidence of post-operative vomiting and nausea, but found it impossible to obtain accurate information; what the patients said did not tie up with what was on the records. Dumas and Leonard, in their study of post-operative vomiting (1963), had to make special arrangements for it to be recorded on the charts to ensure the validity of their data.

If the data sources for the project were unreliable, it could lead to spurious results. In the end, we used a variety of sources, but for the important outcome measures we obtained information directly from the patients but this was not always as accurate as one might expect. The psychological literature is full of examples of the subjectivity of data from people.

Timing

We wanted to collect information at two stages in patients' recovery: firstly while the patient was still in hospital and secondly, once they had been discharged. It was important to consider *when* the measurement of outcome should take place. Measurements may change over time, previous responses may influence a second response. Research looking at pain, for example, shows that a single outcome measurement of pain is unreliable as an indication of general experience of pain, as it is quite possible that a patient may just have had a dose of analgesia. The general level of pain, therefore, would be greatly underestimated. Similarly, a measurement comparing degrees of recovery would be inaccurate unless the time of administration is standardized. Patients' pain on the second post-operative day may be different from pain on their fourth post-operative day.

We ran a pilot study to identify the best times to contact patients and found that the third post-operative day was the best time whilst patients were still in hospital. In choosing this day we obviously missed all those patients who were discharged earlier. However, the pilot showed us that if we chose the second post-operative day, a number of patients were too tired or ill to answer the questions.

It was possible that the effects of DySSSy would not be seen immediately and so we contacted patients postally at a specified post-operative date. Trying to get patients to fill in a questionnaire which arrives in the post on a *specific day* was not easy. Some patients did not respond for months, meaning that their recovery information was totally invalid!

Timing can be important for other reasons as well. Regarding the measurement of satisfaction, it has been found that high levels of satisfaction are typically reported by hospital in-patients. Patients are often reluctant to complain due to fears of reprisal if they criticize their carers whilst still dependent on them in hospital. To reduce patients' fears of reprisal, post-discharge data collection is often recommended. This is what we did for the ODySSSy Project.

Confounding with the experiment

Confounding of results by the experiment itself is not uncommon. One example of this is the 'Hawthorne effect' which describes how the experimental *process* rather than the intervention itself may affect the results. We had lengthy discussions on how to limit this, including the possibility of the control wards meeting regularly to discuss a Christmas party. Both wards did receive similar attention in terms of data collector activity, but not in terms of facilitation. Our only defence is that group work and facilitation are an integral part of standard setting and to try, in this project, to tease out which bits of DySSSy were effective was really a bit ambitious: the subject of a whole new project, no doubt!

Another problem is where the measurements might be affected by the experiment in an unexpected way. This is illustrated in studies by both Boore (1978) and Davis (1984). They found an unexpected contamination of their outcome by the actual process they were trying to evaluate. Analgesia consumption was taken as a measure of outcome and a reduction in analgesia consumption was taken as an indicator of improved recovery. In both cases, the intervention being assessed was preoperative information giving and this teaching encouraged patients to ask for more analgesia if they were in pain. The consequence was an increase in analgesia consumption by the patients who had undergone the intervention that was supposed to reduce it.

If an experimental ward is next door to a control ward, it may well be that nurses and patients will swap between wards. Even mere socializing can ruin an experiment. Nurses could talk about the experiment they are involved in to other nurses in the control ward. The control ward might then change their behaviour or start up an experiment themselves, especially if the intervention being tested appears to have a beneficial effect. This is known as an 'interaction effect'. In the ODySSSy Project we tried to avoid this happening by ensuring that experimental and control wards within the same hospital were far apart from each other and had minimum interaction. We also excluded all patients who were moved onto the ward from another ward.

Experimenter bias

There is always a risk that the experimenter themselves may introduce bias to the data collected and thus confound the results. This can be done either consciously or unconsciously. An experimenter who is wedded to a particular idea or hypothesis may be reluctant to drop it even though the data may not support the hypothesis. Paul Broca, mentioned at the beginning of this chapter, is a case in point. He was so convinced that sexual, racial and social differences in brain size determined intelligence that he selected the factors he included in any analyses so that this hypothesis stood up. Here bias crept into the interpretation rather than the acquisition of data.

We had to be especially careful. As well as being responsible for evaluating DySSSy, the Royal College of Nursing actually developed the system. In this respect, as evaluators, we had to be very careful throughout the project to prevent our feelings about DySSSy influencing the way we collected and interpreted the data. From a data collection point of view, we employed five local data collectors in the five hospital sites who were blind to the experiment (i.e. which wards were setting standards and which were controls). It would be difficult to say whether they remained blind to the experiment throughout the whole study – you would probably need a blind, deaf and dumb data collector to do that!

CONCLUSIONS

We tried hard to overcome some of the problems of confounding in relation to outcome measurement in the ODySSSy Project. I doubt that we succeeded entirely but at least we gave it our best. Being *aware* of confounding and measurement issues is probably the most important thing. Outcomes of care are affected by many processes – individual, social, organizational, situational – and any attempt to compare outcomes in relation to a particular process will fail to produce significant results or will produce spurious results if these other processes remain uncontrolled or unrecognized. Not every evaluation is going to be problematic. The kinds of factors which may confound results will vary according to the project and its design. In reality, it is probably impossible to think of everything that will affect results, but at least by considering the major confounding variables, we hope that the research conclusions arising from the ODySSSy Project at least are more likely to be well founded.

Health services research often forms the basis for health policy. If a nursing intervention in a research project is found to be beneficial, it may well be implemented on a larger scale elsewhere. Ill-founded conclusions and recommendations may have costly repercussions. The conclusions of the craniometricians of the last century may sound amusing to us today, but their work formed the basis of what Gould terms 'scientific racism' and sexism – a justification for hierarchy and repression. If their theories still stood today, women might not have the vote. Confounding in research must be addressed to help us leap to the right conclusions. Leaping to the wrong conclusions may have unforeseen consequences!

Acknowledgements

The author would like to acknowledge the Department of Health Nursing Division for the funding of the ODySSSy Project and the other members of the ODySSSy Project Team.

REFERENCES

Bloch, D. (1980) Interrelated issues in evaluation and evaluation research. *Nursing Research*, **29**(2), 69–73.

Boore, J.R.P. (1978) *Prescription for Recovery*, Royal College of Nursing, London.

Buck, N., Devlin, H.B., and Lunn, J.N. (1987) *Report of a Confidential Enquiry into Perioperative Death*, The Nuffield Provincial Hospitals Trust/The King's Fund, London.

Bucquet, D. and Curtis, S. (1986) Socio-demographic variation in perceived illness and the use of primary care: the value of community survey data for primary care service planning. *Social Science and Medicine*, **23**(7), 737–44.

Davis, B.D. (1984) *Preoperative Information Giving and Patients' Postoperative Outcomes: An Implementation Study*. Report prepared for the Scottish Home and Health Department, Department of Nursing studies, Edinburgh University.

Dumas, R.G. and Leonard, R.C. (1963) The effect of nursing on the incidence of post-operative vomiting. *Nursing Research*, **12**(1), 12–15.

Gould, S.J. (1981) *The Mismeasure of Man*, Penguin, London.

Hegyvary, S.T. and Haussman, R.K.D. (1976a) The relationship of nursing process and patient outcomes. *Journal of Nursing Administration*, **6**(9), 18–21.

Hegyvary, S.T. and Haussman, R.K.D. (1976b) Nursing professional review. *Journal of Nursing Administration*, **6**(9), 12–16.

Horn, B.J. (1980) Establishing valid and reliable criteria. *Nursing Research*, **29**(2), 88–90.

Johnston, M. (1986) Preoperative emotional states and postoperative recovery, in *Psychological Aspects of Surgery*, (ed. F.G. Guggenheim), Karger, Basel.

Le Bon, G. (1879) Recherches anatomiques et mathématiques sur les lois des variations du volume du cerveau et sur leurs relations avec l'intelligence. *Revue d'Anthropologie*, 2nd series, **2**, 27–104, quoted in Gould, S.J. (1981) *The Mismeasure of Man*, Penguin, London.

Mathews, A. and Ridgeway, V. (1981) Personality and recovery from surgery. *British Journal of Clinical Psychology*, **20**, 243–60.

McGhee, A. (1961) *The Patients' Attitude to Nursing Care*, E. and S. Livingstone, Edinburgh.

Pollard, W.E., Bobbitt, R.A. and Bergner, M. (1978) Examination of variable errors of measurement in a survey-based social indicator. *Social Indicators Research*, **5**, 279–301.

Robinson, J., Strong, P. and Elkan, R. (1989) *Griffiths and the Nurses: a National Survey of CNAs*, Nursing Policy Studies Centre, University of Warwick.

Royal College of Nursing Standards of Care Project (1990) *Quality Patient Care: the Dynamic Standard Setting System*, Royal College of Nursing, London.

Salmon, P. (1985) Cures and curiosities. *Times Health Supplement*, 5th December.

Starfield, B. (1974) Measurement of outcome: a proposed scheme. *Health and Society*, **Winter**, 39–50.

Townsend, P. and Davidson, N. (1982) *Inequalities in Health*, Penguin, London.

Weiss, G.L. (1988) Patient satisfaction with primary medical care. Evaluation of sociodemographic and predispositional factors. *Medical Care*, **26**(4), 383–92.

Williamson, J.W. (1971) Evaluating quality of patient care. *Journal of the American Medical Association*, **218**(4), 564–9.

11

Research for whom? The politics of research dissemination and application

Jane Robinson

INTRODUCTION

Research methodologies abound in prescriptive, normative statements about how research should or should not be done. Indeed the function of most social science methods texts is to provide recipes for doing social research – and such texts are known in the trade as cookbooks. Yet all practising researchers know that social research is not like it is presented and prescribed in those texts. It is infinitely more complex, messy, various and much more interesting. These accounts do, of course, also expose the soft underbelly of social science – unprotected by the hard shell of quantitative science as normally presented to the world through those texts, books and monographs. That social science also takes place in a political context you would never guess from the methodology texts.

(*Bell and Encel, 1978, pp. 4–5*)

The text from which the above quotation is taken was one of a series of edited collections which greatly helped me to make sense of the research experience to be described in this chapter. All of the authors included in the series struck me with their unashamed honesty about what doing social research (especially contract research) is *really* like. The other crucial texts included *Doing Sociological Research* (Bell and Newby, 1981), *Social Researching – Politics, Problems, Practice* (Bell and Roberts, 1984) and *Doing Feminist Research* (Roberts, 1981). How, I reflected, these accounts differed from the standard nursing research cookbooks with their preoccupation with technique and process – both apparently completely divorced from the personal, social and cultural identities of the researchers and the researched! Most of what was and is written concerning nursing research contains virtually nothing about the problems and the fascination of how we come to describe and to know the social world of which we are intrinsically a part. I was therefore delighted to receive an invitation to contribute this chapter to a book which promises to begin to set the record straight on nursing research.

The subject matter of the chapter arose from some teaching which I contributed to the MA in the Sociology of Health and Healing at the University of Warwick during the mid-1980s. One of the editors of this current edition (Richard McMahon) was a student member of that course. The messages which I tried then to convey must have struck a chord for in 1991, approximately five years later, he offered me the opportunity to record in this book some of the research experiences which I had related to his class. In trying to recall the flavour of those two sessions on policy research in health care it seemed, with all the benefits of hindsight, that I had been concerned to inject a note of caution and of realism into the whole business of applied research. In contributing to that MA course I remember feeling that I would be doing less than justice to the part time mature students (the majority of whom were nurses) if I did not sensitize them (as they embarked perhaps for the first time on a piece of research of their own) to some of the problems and the pitfalls which I had encountered as an emerging health policy analyst who also happened to be a nurse.

THE RESEARCH IN CONTEXT

At the time of those teaching sessions at Warwick I was still reeling from the impact of carrying out a highly sensitive piece of participant observation research into the problem of perinatal mortality in one health authority and I had recently been awarded a PhD (Robinson, 1986) for my account of that research experience – an account which included a multilevel description of the research context, process and product. The original research report had, however, never been published for it had been embargoed in October 1983 by the chairman of the commissioning health authority upon its one and only presentation to the closed session of a meeting of health authority members.

My reactions to this turn of events were intensely ambivalent. On the one hand they encompassed feelings of anger and grief at my powerlessness to be able to use the lessons of the research findings in order to bring about change on behalf of the parents whose babies had died and who had participated so willingly in the research process. Medical power had never seemed so omnipotent as when I realized that despite having uncovered aspects of care which raised questions about the management of some pregnancies, no one was required to consider the implications of the findings for their own professional practice. Paradoxically, on the other hand, I also felt a sense of worthlessness and guilt that I had caused hurt and upset to members of health authority staff (especially medical staff) who, like the parents, had also participated willingly in the research and who had given me open access to meetings and to medical records. This is not to suggest that nothing was achieved. As the following account shows, a working party was convened and an attempt was made to address the issues which the research raised. Yet much of the energy of that working party was devoted to denying the validity of the research observations and therefore to not accepting the need to recognize that there really was a problem about which something could be done.

One of the net results of these ambivalent feelings of impotent anger and guilt was that I found it extraordinarily painful to go back over my data in order to undertake the analyses of the policy perspectives arising from the study which were needed for the completion of the PhD. For a year I could hardly bring myself to contemplate the work and even then it was only because other people put strong pressure on me and lent me their support that the thesis itself was eventually completed. Publications proved to be equally difficult to produce, although slowly they began to emerge and over time progressed to show an interesting transition from the detail of the empirical study to the more general lessons which could be learnt from it (Robinson, 1987, 1989a, 1989b; Robinson and Allison, 1991).

REFLEXIVITY IN SOCIAL RESEARCH

It took a long period of deep personal reflection and analysis in order to understand and to come to terms with these reactions. Eventually I came to realize that such reflexivity is itself a crucial part of both the research and the learning processes which arise from it. As a result of that reflection I can now assert with reasonable confidence that feelings of guilt in situations of this nature appear to represent part of a subordination process in which the bearer of bad news is made to feel unworthy and mistaken in their conclusions. The focus of attention and the onus of proof shifts from the recipients to the bearer of the unwelcome message. In a phrase – 'If you don't like the message, shoot the messenger'. This phenomenon is now well documented in cases of 'whistle-blowing' (News Focus, 1991) but is not usually articulated in the context of research findings. This omission is a serious indictment of how research methodology and application are taught to nurses although it may help to explain why nurses so often appear to take refuge in the myth of objectivity and detachment in social research. Arguably the absence of such discussion in the context of nursing research also seriously misleads neophyte researchers into believing that research application is a simple and straightforward matter.

In the account which follows I do not believe that as a researcher I was particularly unusual or exceptional. Where I did perhaps differ was in my subsequent reactions to the experience. However painful the reflective process may have been it resulted in my becoming determined not to accept at face value the initial reactions to the research findings but to try instead to understand and to explain the phenomena. The lessons I learnt were concerned with the social and political aspects of applied research. At one level it seems perfectly obvious that if new knowledge challenges the status quo then its application will be concerned with issues of power and control. At another level it throws into question all of the current preoccupations with audit in the National Health Service and with how change is ever brought about within organizations. It is the detail of how these issues worked out in practice within one research project which I shall try to make explicit in this chapter.

The remainder of the chapter is in two parts. First, the main issues arising from the empirical research are described as a case study. Space dictates, however, that this section can only be used to convey the most minimal description of what was, in reality, an enormously detailed and complex piece of work encompassing in total two action packed years from 1981 to 1983 and then the slower part time process of writing up the PhD which took until the end of 1985. The main purpose of what I shall describe here of the actual study is to try to answer the criticisms which were received from some members of medical staff that the research findings were inaccurate. Obviously this is criticism which has to be taken seriously. For more detailed information on the broader aspects of the research the reader is directed to the original thesis (Robinson, 1986). In the second and final part of the chapter, the lessons which I have drawn from the research and which are touched on in this introductory section are developed and discussed.

THE EMPIRICAL RESEARCH

In September 1981 I was appointed to a research post in a district health authority medical department which included the following remarkable (some would say impossible) job description:

The Research Officer is directly accountable to the District Medical Officer for the research of health problems within 'A' Health Authority in order that operational and strategic plans reflect an understanding of health care and preventive medicine needs of the community. The principal task is to introduce more precise information on the problem of perinatal mortality in order that speculative planning is reduced to the minimum. The job is concerned with the gathering and analysis of data directly from clients/patients and from health service professionals.

He/she will be responsible for the following main functions:

a) To undertake interviews with patients/clients and professional staff in order to gather and analyse data relating to the medical, biological, social, educational, cultural and environmental factors in perinatal mortality in 'A' Health Authority.

Further clauses followed which included:

- monitoring the effects of changing policies on perinatal mortality;
- developing links with health care researchers at university, polytechnic and regional health Authority levels;
- liaising with all disciplines of staff including the Planning and Information Officer;
- contributing to in-service education for a range of professionals on the implications of the research in both general and specific terms;
- generating articles on the subject of in-house research;
- undertaking similar research in other fields.

Although apparently daunting in its scope I was delighted with the opportunities which this broadbased research job offered and within the context of planning, carrying out and writing up a one year empirical study of perinatal mortality, I have no doubt that all of the objectives of that job description were fulfilled. I had had experience of two earlier pieces of research with strong policy implications, although neither was contract research (Robinson, 1979, 1980, 1982). I was absorbed already by the methodological and political problems which appear to be inherent in much policy research and also by the analytical possibilities offered through a critical approach to policy issues (Rein, 1976; Hall *et al.*, 1978; Bulmer, 1982). I wanted to explore these issues further and if I needed further motivation to take the post it was that as a polytechnic (health visitor) lecturer I was intensely frustrated by the then lack of opportunity for personal research. I therefore resigned my lectureship and threw myself with excitement and enthusiasm into the challenges offered by this innovative health authority research job.

With the support of my new employers I registered simultaneously for a PhD in a university Department of Social Anthropology, Social Work and Social Policy on the understanding that I would use the empirical research as a case study of the policy implications of applied research. Despite my earlier research experience I had no anticipation that those implications would be quite so politically sensitive. I was assured of social research supervision through my supervisor Professor Olive Stevenson and I immediately set about negotiating support for the epidemiological aspects of the study. In this I was fortunate to have the interest and guidance of a professor of social medicine whose research into large volumes of historical data on perinatal mortality was to mirror some of the issues which I subsequently identified tentatively at a microscopic level (Knox, Lancashire and Armstrong, 1986). (These issues centre around the possibility of identifying un-explained variations in the performance of different obstetric units by excluding from the data certain classes of birth and on indirect standardization for birthweight.) I was also given complete freedom to seek advice on methodological issues from a range of experts in the field, the most notable of whom were based at the National Perinatal Epidemiology Unit (NPEU) – a recently established Department of Health Research Unit – at the Radcliffe Infirmary, Oxford. It was their recommendations for research methods for local perinatal surveys which I was to follow to the letter in my study (NPEU, 1978).

The question of whether or not my findings were correct hinges on the validity of the research outcomes for each of the NPEU's four recommended inclusion criteria. Because this is such a central issue I shall discuss each in some depth together with relevant aspects of the research findings. The research methods recommended for inclusion by the NPEU were as follows:

1. All perinatal deaths within a geographically defined population

In the study referred to here this was represented by all the deaths (77) occurring between 1 January and 31 December 1982 to mothers resident within the health authority geographical boundary. This methodological device ensured that the total number of health authority births during the same period (4249) could then be used as a denominator, giving a local district perinatal mortality rate in 1982 of 18.1 per 1000 total births. Once these data were established it was then possible to identify what proportion of births to health authority resident mothers took place in different obstetric units. For example, 2428 (57%) of authority resident mothers were confined in the district maternity unit where, however, 54 (70%) of the deaths oc-curred. 1524 (35.9%) of births and the remaining 23 (30%)

of deaths took place in three other cross-boundary hospitals. Domiciliary confinements and other hospitals accounted for the remaining 297 (7.0%) of births and there were no deaths in this latter group.

This simple but crucial aspect of epidemiological research (i.e. using a geographical population as the denominator) enables careful comparisons to be made between the characteristics and experiences of different subpopulations and eliminates the unavoidable and uninvestigatable bias which is built into studies confined to *hospital* populations. (The bias is uninvestigatable because you cannot know the boundaries and therefore the characteristics of the *total* populations from which hospitals draw their patients.) If, however, you know the distribution of certain characteristics within the total geographically defined population (the denominator) then their distribution can be compared with the same characteristics within the numerator (total perinatal deaths within that population). For example, birthweight data, which should be routinely available for all health authority births, are invaluable for such comparisons in the case of perinatal mortality.

Some detail has been given about the justification for this particular aspect of the methodology because at the end of the study some of the most bitter recriminations centred around the ways in which the babies who died were born to mothers who were 'different' to those who survived. Some medical consultants subscribed to the view that the high perinatal mortality rates experienced in their health authority arose from differences in the characteristics of the mothers for whom they were responsible (namely, that more of them came from ethnic minority groups, were poorer, less well educated, irresponsible in lifestyles and in their use of medical services than the mothers of surviving babies). They claimed, furthermore, that the health authority resident mothers who used 'their' hospital were more materially disadvantaged and booked later for antenatal care than those using the other hospitals.

These claims were not easy either to substantiate or disprove because of the unreliability of some of the data sources on which one had to depend. In particular, Hospital Activity Data which should, in theory, have provided data on numerous categories of evidence for the total population of births (including data on service utilization and medical interventions) were found to be so incomplete as to be totally unreliable. Only data on birthweight distribution by place of birth and maternal geographical area of residence were ultimately obtained for *all* births using the Statutory Notification of Births as a data source.

Nevertheless this provided evidence that there were no significant differences in birthweight distribution between the different hospitals in the study. Indeed, if national and regional policy had been followed to the letter, one would have expected greater variation between the hospitals arising from the selection of mothers at risk of premature birth for confinement in centres with neonatal intensive care facilities.

2. The generation of an appropriate control group

As stated above, in an ideal world the total population of health authority births would have been used as a denominator for a whole range of variables. However, having exhausted the potential of the data which is available for the total population, a control group provides an alternative sample population which can be used to generate further data for comparative purposes. Although the NPEU made this recommendation, no further guidance was given as to which variables to control for in the matching process between cases and controls. Surprisingly too, given the tremendous reliance on case–control trials in epidemiological research, there was very little guidance on the question of matching in the literature. In general, there appeared to be an assumption that in perinatal research one controlled for factors such as age of mother, parity, social class and ethnicity. However, once these variables are matched between cases and controls they are then eliminated from any subsequent statistical analysis and this may mask important local idiosyncrasies. For example, I wanted to test out the assumption that the mothers whose babies died (the cases) were different from those whose babies survived (the controls) for a range of social, demographic and economic variables. If I had matched the social class, ethnicity, marital status and age of the control mothers with those of the case mothers, then I would have had no way of knowing whether there was any difference between the cases and the controls in these important respects. Indeed, because a vital aspect of any research lies in the nature of the questions that are selected for asking, if certain questions are eliminated by virtue of assuming *a priori* that the answers are self-evident then an important element of bias is introduced into the research infrastructure.

I consulted widely on this aspect of the methodology and concluded, somewhat arrogantly, that no one had got it *exactly* right! One perinatal epidemiologist had thought very much along the same lines and in the end a modified form of the matching used in his study was adopted (Clarke and Clayton, 1981). This involved taking the infant of the same sex born immediately prior to the perinatal death in the mother's intended place of confinement *at the time of the first antenatal booking*. The rationale behind this lay in the assumption that mothers of comparative obstetric risk would be matched – high risk mothers being booked for consultant units, lower risk mothers for general practitioner units. One could then trace the pregnancy 'careers' of the mothers through the various forms of obstetric care.

In the event, this form of matching was not ideal because 95% of mothers were booked for consultant units. Nevertheless it did enable important comparisons to be made between the units where it was discovered that policies for antenatal and intrapartum care were markedly different. It also enabled a challenge to be made to the *a priori* assumption that the mothers whose babies died were different from the control mothers on a range of social and economic variables, for *no* statistically significant differences were identified. In fact, the *total* case–control population was found to be relatively disadvantaged (for example, 25% of *all* fathers were unemployed compared with 17.2% of all males aged 16–64 in the authority for the 1981 census). The effects of the economic recession were relatively severe in the indigenous population who were mainly from social class III manual occupations and some of whose male members had recently been made redundant from heavy industries.

The number of deaths (31%) to mothers from ethnic minorities appeared to be high in comparison to the proportion in the indigenous population (11.4% from the New Commonwealth and Pakistan in the 1981 census); but not in comparison with their controls. There was an almost equal distribution of case and control mothers from ethnic minorities in each of the hospitals in the study. This distribution appeared to be representative of the varied proportions of ethnic minority mothers using the different obstetric units. However, in the absence of an appropriate population denominator for births to all residents by ethnic group the validity of this observation could not be tested. This finding was also undoubtedly skewed to some extent by variations in the age distribution between the ethnic and indigenous populations. The ethnic minority groups not only had larger proportions of younger people of childbearing age but also experienced higher fertility rates than the indigenous population. The excess of observed over expected deaths appeared to lie in the large number of lethal congenital malformations occurring amongst the ethnic minority mothers. Once again, the absence of appropriate denominator data meant that the validity of this observation could not be tested.

There were 11 illegitimate babies amongst the cases, eight amongst the controls. Eleven of the mothers (six cases and five controls) were living in apparently stable cohabitation and three were single mothers living with their own parents. Just two were living in apparently unstable social circumstances. One was a high risk mother who was in regular contact with health and social workers. Nevertheless she was the only mother in the whole survey to have concealed her pregnancy and to have received no antenatal care. (She proved highly elusive and was never interviewed properly even though I helped with the baby's funeral arrangements, including transporting the mother to hospital and to the Registrar.) For the remainder, antenatal attendance varied only slightly from the population of legitimate pregnancies. This variety in social circumstances was a powerful reminder that legally defined illegitimacy is a relatively common contemporary occurrence. Nevertheless, these births predominated amongst young mothers aged 18–19 years and evidence from the interviews suggested that the stigma associated with illegitimacy persists and that this led, on occasions, to very serious breakdowns in communication between health care professionals and the mothers themselves.

Differences in maternal age and total number of previous pregnancies between cases and controls were statistically significant ($p = 0.05$ and $p = 0.01$ respectively). These are well known indicators of increased obstetric risk and mothers in these groups should, in theory, experience increased antenatal care and surveillance but this was not always apparently the case.

One third of case mothers smoked during pregnancy compared with one fifth of controls (not significant, $p = 0.07$). While 13 (17%) of case mothers stated that they smoked more than 16 cigarettes a day before the pregnancy, four claimed to have reduced consumption or given up once pregnant. In total, 25 (32%) case mothers compared with 16 controls smoked during pregnancy. Although undoubtedly worrying, these numbers were substantially less than was widely believed by health care professionals. Indeed it was later suggested that the mothers lied about this information.

There was little evidence of mothers deliberately refraining from booking antenatal care. By 18 weeks 84.3% of cases and 85.7% of controls had attended their GP and 78% of both populations had attended hospital for the first time. A small proportion of mothers had not by then arrived in the United Kingdom or were in the Indian subcontinent on holiday.

It was concluded that no clearcut picture between cases and controls emerged for a range of social, maternal and access to services variables. The overwhelming impression was of a group of mothers many of whom (but not all) experienced some form of social and physiological disadvantage (estimated in the survey by maternal height, weight, haemoglobin estimation and morbidity in pregnancy); some lost their babies, others did not. Once in the health care system the service which some of the mothers received gave rise to more concern. This population, which was disadvantaged on a number of measures, did not always appear to receive the compensatory forms of health care recommended by the Short Committee (House of Commons, 1980). The overall picture of investigations carried out during pre-, intra- and postpartum care was of a very limited use of screening techniques and/or technological intervention even in cases where there was uncertainty about dates, maternal morbidity and/or a family history of premature labour or congenital malformation. For example seven mothers received alphafetoprotein estimation (146 did not, one (case) had amniocentesis) and 44.2% of cases did not have an ultrasound examination. The report did not suggest that these procedures should be performed routinely, it merely noted that different hospitals apparently followed different policies.

Further differences in medical intervention and attitudes were observed between staff in the four hospitals. For example, three complicating factors during labour – spontaneous rupture of membranes with delayed labour onset, intrapartum haemorrhage and abnormal presentation – showed highly significant differences between cases and controls. Although such differences are predictable (these complications are inevitably associated with an increase in perinatal deaths) there were variations in the response to them by medical staff in different hospitals in the study.

Forty seven (62%) of the deaths occurred in apparently normally formed infants weighing 1000 g and above and standardization by birthweight showed that there was an excess of observed over expected deaths in the heavier birthweight band of 2501 g and above.

Nineteen (25%) of the deaths were in babies with identified congenital malformations. Nine of these were neural tube defects which together with five survivors beyond the first week of life gave a district rate of 3.29 per 1000 births compared with 1.92 for England and Wales (1981). (This was apparently related, in part, to the absence of routine screening procedures for these conditions.)

The district perinatal rate was 6.8 points above the rate for England and Wales. Nevertheless, just two babies (both cases) were delivered by a consultant obstetrician. Consultant obstetricians were not present at any of the remaining deliveries. Twenty nine cases and 19 controls were delivered by an obstetric registrar or SHO; 44 and 56 respectively by midwives. No cases or controls had a consultant anaesthetist or paediatrician present at the delivery. Eighteen cases and ten controls had a paediatric registrar or Senior House Officer present.

All of the information referred to in this section was generated for both cases and controls and was obtained via the two remaining research methods recommended by NPEU which are described below.

3. A minimum data set suggested by NPEU for use by all researchers surveying perinatal death

An 18 page questionnaire was eventually developed encompassing (with some modifications) the NPEU recommended minimum data set plus a range of questions derived from additional sources. The questionnaire was completed mainly from medical records. Where necessary clarification was sought from parental interviews, health care professionals and from attendance at the perinatal review meetings held to review individual cases in each of the hospitals. (The latter varied widely in form and content and this aspect of management was eventually incorporated in the final report and in the PhD thesis.)

4. Information sought from the mother, preferably in her own home

Seventy five case and 73 control (a total of 96%) mothers, and many of the fathers, were interviewed; a sad experience which revealed many unexpected facets of the situation. For example, the funerals of dead babies had proved to be very traumatic for many and a relatively expensive procedure for several parents (Robinson, 1987). Some of the mothers had harrowing stories to tell (not confined to cases) of seeking help when there was a feeling that all was not well, of powerlessness in the face of medical 'expertise' and of the intransigence of some doctors in their refusal to take seriously the mother's account of events.

Participant observation as a health authority employee attending perinatal review meetings, maternity liaison group meetings and interviewing the parents of cases and controls led to the conclusion that inequality lay not so much in the characteristics of the population whose babies died as in the treatment they or their mothers received. Attempts on the part of parents, especially mothers, to participate in their care or to communicate their worries that all was not well with their pregnancy were 'put down' by some members of medical staff. This behaviour was justified on the grounds that the mothers were either too ill educated or so irresponsible that they could not possibly know what was happening to them. On occasions quite blatant racism and 'classism' were observed.

Yet doctors working in the hospital where the largest proportion of deaths occurred were hardworking and committed. There were severe shortages of medical and midwifery staff; they worked in the shadow of a regional centre of excellence; and they had to cope with the persistent stigma of relatively high perinatal mortality rates. Nevertheless the authoritarian and didactic attitudes which were observed led them to 'blame the victims' rather than to examine possible modifications of their practice and to seek amelioration of staffing problems. It was concluded that technological intervention might possibly have led to a satisfactory outcome in some cases (or screened out lethal malformations) but parents generally did not have the choice. It was the absence of choice, of any feeling of partnership in care, which gave a sense of real poverty to the services which some of these parents experienced. Inequality in health meant nothing to them in terms of impersonal collective categories such as ethnicity, class or marital status. Inequality on their terms was the reality of poverty, of losing your baby, of not being able to afford the funeral and sometimes being treated as if you were feckless or stupid or uncaring. Worst of all, it could mean being denied the right to be listened to even when what you had to say might just have altered completely the subsequent course of events.

Subsequent study arising from the empirical evidence for the completion of the PhD led to the development of explanations for the phenomena encountered in this study. For example, detailed examination of the Registrar General's annual statistical reports from the 1940s onwards and of several major inquiries into maternity services and perinatal death led to the conclusion that perinatal mortality is almost invariably constructed in official statistics in such a way as to highlight the significance of social and maternal characteristics rather than the possible influence of medical care (Joint Committee, 1948; Joint Committee, 1949; Butler and Bonham, 1963; Butler and Alberman, 1969; Chamberlain et al., 1975; Chamberlain et al., 1978; DHSS, 1980; House of Commons, 1980, 1984).

The analysis of the 'social construction' of mortality rates lends powerful support to the idea that medical education leads to the socialization of some doctors to see perinatal mortality in maternal, economic and social terms for successive medical reports on the problem have emphasized sometimes in subtle and sometimes quite direct ways the victims' contribution to the failed pregnancy (Armstrong, 1986; Robinson and Allison, 1991).

Finally, it was hypothesized that women in medicine have to fight so hard to reach the top in their careers that (paradoxically) they may become even more didactic than male doctors (as was observed in the study).

EARLY LESSONS FROM THE RESEARCH EXPERIENCE

This study of perinatal mortality in one health authority demonstrated unequivocally the complex and often contentious nature of research which exposes hidden assumptions and explores them in a systematic way. Work of this nature (although written extremely carefully and never claiming more from the evidence than could reasonably be deduced from a one year study) was inevitably very threatening to the key actors who were directly involved. They reacted with anger and having all the power of the medical profession behind them (including the threat of the Medical Defence Union), insisted that it should only be presented in the strictest confidence to one closed health authority meeting and then embargoed. The chairman charged members with the total confidence of the report and referred it to the Maternity Services Working Party for investigation of its policy implications. I was included in this group and so observation of later developments was possible.

The group processes during the eight months of the Working Party's existence could be divided into roughly three stages. First, there was dissipation of anger and the re-establishment and confirmation of individual and group identities. During this first period the research was attacked systematically as inaccurate yet most of the attacks were oblique, ignoring completely, for example, the hard evidence of the quantitative data. The justification for this non-scientific approach appeared to lie in the fact that as the research worker had been a nurse this exonerated anyone from taking the findings seriously.

The attack was led by a consultant member in the form of a report which ignored the carefully constructed analysis and qualified comments in the original research. A detailed response to the criticisms was presented but was completely ignored by the medical members. Nursing and midwifery members regrettably made no contribution at all, although their privately expressed anxiety about some of the issues which had been raised was common local knowledge. The capacity to ignore the arguments of the research report and to describe the findings as inaccurate was encountered throughout the meetings, although gradually as members were charged by the chairman with specific tasks the overt hostility grew less. One consultant produced a report on obstetric aspects of perinatal death which simply compared a range of subcategories of perinatal death for three (non-health authority) hospitals. The entrenched notion of looking only at hospital populations despite their acknowledged inbuilt biases was reinforced. The idea that the women of the authority were ignorant or feckless was reiterated and, on one occasion, when protesting at the assumptions of irresponsibility which were being implied I repeated the research findings of numerous failures of communication. It was claimed then that even talking to the women 'in words of two syllables' produced no effect.

Following the third meeting of the Working Party the chairman wrote a report for members. It stated that opportunities had been given for discussion of the scientific aspects of the research report and assumptions examined in order that members should be fully briefed before looking at specific programmes of action. The time had now come to decide on the tasks which the Working Party should complete within the time scale. As a way forward it was suggested that effort should be concentrated on those recommendations which could be directly implemented by the health authority and which had practical expression. Each Working Party member was then charged with individual task(s) to be completed within a specific period of time.

In this way the situation was 'moved on' from the catharsis of anger to the constructive aspects of building new policy proposals together with strategies for their implementation. Subject areas included: medical and midwifery staffing levels; perinatal audit; health education and communication; family planning; screening; rubella immunization; counselling; training; provision of services; and the need for improved data collection and for research.

The second stage of the Working Party's lifespan did not produce any utopian change of attitudes. Nevertheless it became apparent that the focus of debate had shifted from the sterile and self-fulfilling defeatism of 'blaming the victims' to an examination of issues which were potentially within members' control.

At first the discussions were pessimistic. Resource constraints within the National Health Service and particularly the then current (1983) review of manpower targets led members to ask how they could possibly expect any improvement in service provision. Under the chairman's guidance, however, it was realized that unless constraints on service provision were made explicit there would be no hope of convincing others of the justice of their case.

As the members produced their individual reports for the Working Party more and more questions came to be asked, for example:

We've always known about the low levels of midwifery staffing – but why do midwives not come and those that do come, leave?

With the present system of shared care for the majority of mothers how can we (the consultants) get to know about low risk mothers who become high risk during pregnancy?

Can we recommend that general practitioners should not see antenatal patients during general surgeries?

Every general practitioner is an independent practitioner, you can't do anything about those who provide bad antenatal care. Can we recommend a midwife to every GP's clinic?

Perhaps the most surprising remark (given the previous hostility) was from the consultant who said:

We need health visitors to sort out the social problems. I'm a doctor – I can't help being a doctor – and inevitably I concentrated on medical factors.

By the time of the seventh meeting sufficient evidence had been produced and collated in order for the chairman to present an interim Working Party report to the health authority. The following four areas were identified and agreed by the authority as having high priority:

- the establishment of a Maternity Services Liaison Committee as recommended in *Maternity Care in Action* (DHSS, 1982); (this involved the acceptance of a lay health authority member as chairman);
- the establishment of a multidisciplinary Perinatal Review Committee;

- the advice given relating to midwifery and medical staffing levels;
- progress in health promotion in the maternity services.

In terms of participant observation this stage represented the conclusion of my connection with the health authority perinatal survey. There had been a movement, at least on paper, from apparent stalemate to a constructive approach to the problems. Preoccupation with social and maternal characteristics had been replaced, through the chairman's insistence, by attention to policy issues which members could at least hope to influence. Deeply held beliefs and attitudes would not change overnight – if at all. It would be during the third stage and beyond that the real evidence of constructive planning might be seen to be implemented. As researcher I was not privileged to observe the outcomes. Just three pieces of information were conveyed privately during the calendar year after my involvement ceased.

The first was a telephone message from the engineer in charge of maintenance of hospital equipment saying that servicing of fetal monitoring equipment was now routine in one of the hospitals. 'Things', he was reported to have said, 'have come out of cupboards that never saw the light of day before you came.' Nevertheless there was reason to believe that this change in practice had more to do with the appointment of new medical staff than with radical changes amongst the old.

Secondly it was learnt that a midwifery sister who had a special interest and training in bereavement counselling had been appointed.

Thirdly a verbal report was received that a consultant had stated that the continuing (relatively) adverse perinatal mortality rate for 1983 was due entirely to socioeconomic factors and that medical care was not implicated in any way!

These three observations appeared to confirm the diffuse and indirect way in which many policy theorists argue that the application of research is achieved. There was no evidence of a direct linear relationship between a recommendation and its implementation. It was abundantly clear that the presentation of knowledge was sufficient to bring about change. It was also necessary for the process to be mediated through the social networks and power structures of role holders in the authority. This process had more to do with professional politics than with the acquisition of research based knowledge. Indeed, the one recommendation which would have ensured the continuing evaluation of trends (the routine collection of statistical information on category of perinatal death by birthweight and place of delivery) was never to my knowledge acted upon.

THE CONCLUDING ANALYSIS FROM THE EMPIRICAL STUDY

Work for the PhD went on to attempt to develop explanations for the phenomena which had been observed. It was concluded that notions of 'causation' in perinatal death could not be separated from the social context in which they were constructed. That context is highly complex and its understanding requires insights into the origins and status of medical expertise; of the place of gender both in medical practice *and* in the ways in which doctors and parent communicate with each other.

Finally, the place of the nurse as researcher in a 'medical' field was explored. It was concluded that the initial, expedient appointment made in the face of public pressure to 'do something' about perinatal mortality and the lack of resources to appoint someone medically qualified had never taken account of a nurse researcher's ability to produce research of this kind. As a result there were profound differences in perception as to what constituted the nurse researcher's role. Therefore, from one point of view, when the findings of the empirical study were denounced as 'inaccurate', it appeared that this verdict was legitimated through being made by doctors whose expertise authorizes them to judge. At a superficial level it was doctors saying 'This nurse is not competent'. From a social constructionist perspective of medical knowledge, however, it epitomized the appropriation of reality by a powerful sector of society. To what extent this situation could be attributed to social class differences, professional hierarchy or rivalry, or the imposition of an authoritarian medical ideology was impossible to judge.

The outcome nevertheless carried implications for policy development in the arena of perinatal mortality. Class, gender and racial discrimination will exist in different manifestations and at different times and may indeed influence individual explanations for phenomena. But this, as Popper (1945) points out, is only to be expected, for we all suffer from our own systems of prejudice. The ultimate lesson of this study was that it is only through the exposure of such individual hypothetical positions to the rigours of replication, falsification and public debate that progress towards scientific explanation can be distinguished from the pseudoscientific, however elegantly it may be disguised as 'expertise'.

LESSONS FOR THE FUTURE

There are several topical policy lessons from this research for nurses which can be extrapolated to the context of current developments in the NHS. Despite current, highly desirable concern with the development of 'audit', in practice the procedures appear to be being focused on (and controlled by) individual professional groups. Yet, as this research demonstrated, there is a tendency to close ranks and to search for alternative explanations whenever a spotlight is turned on to the performance of individual groups of workers, especially if they have the ultimate power to control events. It seems almost inevitable, therefore, that vast sums of money will be spent on going through the *motions* of audit but with no real hope of change in subsequent practice unless the really difficult issue of *change management* is taken on board at the same time.

One major lesson was that if the opportunity arose to go back and do all of the perinatal research again in the light of what has subsequently been learnt, it would be with the intention of carrying out a piece of *true* action research. This would require incorporation into the research methodology of techniques for taking members of staff along with the findings as they arose and for dealing with their feelings of threat and denial. It would need to involve helping them to recognize and to come to terms with their own stereotyped views on the nature of the problem. It would also involve empowering the staff so that they did not feel hopeless and helpless at the prospect of being able to effect structural changes in the management of their service. But all of this would require me *as the researcher* to feel confident to bring about the changes which might have a chance of becoming permanent. Yet, as I have shown, the research experience left me feeling *disempowered* and guilty at the upset I had caused. Which brings me to the final issues arising from this research experience.

No contract researcher should be left unsupported with the awesome responsibility both of doing the research and of handling the highly charged political consequences of the findings. This is a serious lesson for nurses in the context of the current NHS. Many nurses are being appointed to either purchaser or provider health service research and development posts (often with far less research training and academic supervision than I enjoyed). Without that crucial element of support many of them may come to feel that they have been set up to fail. Their immediate employers need to understand their own crucial responsibilities in ensuring first that the focus and methodology of the studies they ask for are appropriate for the questions which need to be asked and, second, that they then back the researcher all the way through the research. Structures of power and hierarchy in health care are unlikely to be swept away. Nurses need to learn to recognize them for what they are and to develop the self-confidence to manage them. This is just as important during the process of carrying out research as in any other form of organizational life.

Academic supervisors of nurse research students also need to reflect on these issues for research teaching and supervision. The majority of nurse students for higher degrees are similar to those who I taught on the Warwick MA. They are mature and experienced professionals who look to research education to provide them with rigorous and systematic techniques in order to address the specific problems which they face in their work situations. They will often wish to research issues for their dissertations such as workload measurement, the organization of nursing work and quality assurance in health care – all issues which are likely to bring political consequences in their train. Will the day ever arise when we shall see a research supervisor or manager answering charges at the UKCC that they are in breach of the Nurses' and Midwives' Professional Code of Conduct because of failure to support a researcher in the dissemination and application of research findings? This is not as extreme a scenario as it may sound, for the whole ethos claimed to lie behind the current NHS reforms is that they will improve standards in health care and make professionals much more accountable to the customer. After all – for whose benefit are we doing all this research?

REFERENCES

Armstrong, D. (1986) The invention of perinatal mortality. *Sociology of Health and Illness*, **8**, 211–32.

Bell, C. and Encel, S. (1978) *Inside the Whale: Ten Personal Accounts of Social Research*, Pergamon, Australia.

Bell, C. and Newby, H. (1981) *Doing Sociological Research*, George Allen and Unwin, London.

Bell, C. and Roberts, H. (1984) *Social Researching: Politics, Problems, Practice*, Routledge and Kegan Paul, London.

Bulmer, M. (1982) *The Uses of Social Research. Social Investigation in Public Policy-Making*, Contemporary Social Research, No. 3, George Allen and Unwin, London.

Butler, N.R. and Alberman, E.D. (1969) *Perinatal Problems. The Second Report of the 1958 British Perinatal Mortality Survey*, E. and S. Livingstone, Edinburgh.

Butler, N.R. and Bonham, D.G. (1963) *Perinatal Mortality. The First Report of the 1958 British Perinatal Mortality Survey*, E. and S. Livingstone, Edinburgh.

Chamberlain, R., Chamberlain, G., Howlett, B. and Claireaux, A. (1975) *British Births 1970. Volume 1. The First Week of Life*, Heinemann, London.

Chamberlain, G., Phillipp, E., Howlett, B. and Masters, K. (1978) *British Births 1970. Volume 2, Obstetric Care*, Heinemann, London.

Clarke, M. and Clayton, D. (1981) The design and interpretation of case–control studies of perinatal mortality. *American Journal of Epidemiology*, **113**(6), 636–45.

Department of Health and Social Security (1980) *Report of the Working Group on Inequalities in Health* (Chairman, Sir Douglas Black). HMSO, London.

Department of Health and Social Security (1982) *Maternity Care in Action – Part 1*, HMSO, London.

Hall, P., Land, H., Parker, R. and Webb, A. (1978) *Change, Choice and Conflict in Social Policy*, Heinemann, London.

House of Commons (1980) *Second Report from the Social Services Committee, Perinatal and Neonatal Mortality*, HMSO, London.

House of Commons (1984) *Third Report from the Social Services Committee, Perinatal and Neonatal Mortality Report: Follow Up*, HMSO, London.

Joint Committe of the Royal College of Obstetricians and Gynaecologists and the British Paediatric Association (1949) *Neonatal Mortality and Morbidity: Reports on Public Health and Medical Subjects No. 94*, HMSO, London.

Joint Committee of the Royal College of Obstetricians and Gynaecologists and the Population Investigation Committee (1948) *Maternity in*

Great Britain, Oxford University Press, Oxford.

Knox, E.G., Lancashire, R. and Armstrong, E.H. (1986) Perinatal mortality standards: construction and use of a health care performance indicator. *Journal of Epidemiology and Community Health*, **40**(3), 193–204.

National Perinatal Epidemiology Unit (1978) *An Introduction to the National Perinatal Epidemiology Unit and Annual Report for 1978*, Radcliffe Infirmary, Oxford.

News Focus (1991) Whistling down the wind. *Health Services Journal*, **101**(5282), 14.

Popper, K. (1945) Against the sociology of knowledge, reprinted in Miller, D. (ed.) (1983) *A Pocket Popper*, Fontana, London.

Rein, M. (1976) *Social Science and Public Policy*, Penguin, Harmondsworth.

Roberts, H. (1981) *Doing Feminist Research*, Routledge and Kegan Paul, London.

Robinson, J.A. (1979) Inter-disciplinary in-service education (for health visitors and social workers). *Child Abuse and Neglect*, **3**, 749–55.

Robinson, J.A. (1980) An evaluation of health visiting: a study of the relevance of historical and theoretical perspectives, and of its impact upon clients' perceptions and usage of the service. University of Keele. Dissertation.

Robinson, J.A. (1982) *An Evaluation of Health Visiting*, CETHV/ENB, London.

Robinson, J.A. (1986) A study of the policy implications arising from a local survey of perinatal mortality. University of Keele. Dissertation.

Robinson, J.A. (1987) A casket instead of a crib. *Senior Nurse*, **7**(1), 16–18.

Robinson, J.A. (1989a) Perinatal mortality – report on a research study. *International Journal of Health Care Quality Assurance*, **2**(2), 13–19.

Robinson, J.A. (1989b) The role of the social sciences in evaluating perinatal care, in *Effective Care in Pregnancy and Childbirth*, (eds. I. Chalmers, M. Enkin, and M.J. Keirse), Oxford University Press, Oxford.

Robinson, J.A., and Allison, J. (1991) *The Social Construction of Perinatal Mortality: A Case Study of Power Relationship between Primary and Secondary Care Obstetrics*. Paper given at the International Conference on Primary Care Obstetrics and Perinatal Health, S'Hertogenbosch, The Netherlands, 21–22 March 1991. In press.

Index

Page numbers appearing in **bold** refer to figures and page numbers appearing in *italic* refer to tables.

Choosing a research
question 17–20
Clinical trials, see Randomized
controlled trials
Coding of interviews 136–40
Collection of data
confounding variables 158–9,
160–61
pilot studies 72–3, 74, 76
triangulation **119**, 124
Confidentiality 105
Confounding factors 10, 147–63
Consent
informed 106
refusal of
by consultants 12, 95–6
by patients 96
Consistency of
measurements 157
Constant comparative
analysis 132
Constraints on research
from funding agencies 11
time 18, 27, 102–3, 132–3
Consultants, absence of
consent 12, 95–6
Continuing care nurses 115
Contradictions
in action research 34–5
in research process 13, 120–24
Control groups
action research 42
interaction effect 160
perinatal mortality 173–7
Control of research
experimental 84–5
by funding agencies 11
Correlational research 85–6
Creativity
in research process 12–14
accessing hidden samples 61
as research question 19–28
tests 24–5, 27
Criteria, research 171–80
randomized controlled
trials 96–7, 97
Criticisms of research
results 180–81
Cross-section sampling 51

Data
access to 54
analysis
creativity in nursing 24–5
pilot studies 78
qualitative 131–46
randomized controlled
trials 93
triangulation 128–9
collection
confounding variables 158–
9, 160–61
pilot studies 72–3, 74, 76
triangulation **119**, 124
sources 158
Decision making process **142**, 143
Defining the research
question 7–8, 17–29
creativity in research 12
Design, research, see
Methodology, choice of
Development
of instruments 69, **70**
of methodology 43–5
Diaries **79**
Phase 3 **74**, 75–6
Phase 4 **77**, 77–8
Dissemination of research 10,
165–88
action research 12
funding agencies 11
District nurses and carers 101–3
Double blind trials 85
Drug addicts, identifying 51
Dynamic Standard Setting
System (DySSSy) 148–9,
152, 156–7, 159–61

Effects of research results 180–84
Enthusiasm for research 18
Ethics committees
accessing hidden samples 11,
53
choosing a research
question 19, 27
randomized controlled trials 95
screening of participants 11
Ethnicity and control
groups 174–5